IN DEMAND

HOW TO BUILD THE MOST SOUGHT AFTER SKILL SET IN THE NEW WORLD ECONOMY

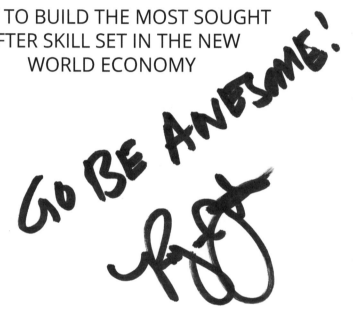

RYAN JATEN

Visit the Official Website at: www.J10.com

Printed in the United States of America

First Printing: October 2021

J10 Holdings LLC.

ISBN-13: 978-0-578-25580-4

Ryan Jaten's books may be purchased for educational, business or sales
promotional use. Special discounts are available on quantity purchases.
For more information, please call or write.

Email: support@j10.com

For orders by U.S. trade bookstores and wholesalers,
please contact us at email address listed above.

DISCLAIMER

The Publisher has strived to be as accurate and complete as possible in the creation of this book. This book is not intended for use as a source of financial advice. All readers are advised to seek services of competent professionals in the financial field.

Readers are cautioned to rely on their own judgment about their individual circumstances to act accordingly.

While all attempts have been made to verify information provided in this publication, the Publisher assumes no responsibility for errors, omissions, or contrary interpretation of the subject matter herein. Any perceived slights of specific persons, peoples, or organizations are unintentional. This book details the author's own personal experiences and opinions. The author is not licensed as a psychologist, or psychiatrist.

The author and publisher are providing this book and its contents on an "as is" basis and make no representations or warranties of any kind with respect to this book or its contents. The author and publisher disclaim all such representations and warranties, including for example warranties of merchantability and educational or medical advice for a particular purpose. In addition, the author and publisher do not represent or warrant that the information accessible via this book is accurate, complete or current.

Except as specifically stated in this book, neither the author or publisher, nor any authors, contributors, or other representatives will be liable for damages arising out of or in connection with the use of this book. This is a comprehensive limitation of liability that applies to all damages of any kind, including (without limitation) compensatory; direct, indirect or direct, indirect or consequential damages; loss of data, income or profit; loss of or damage to property and claims of third parties.

You understand that this book is not intended as a substitute for consultation with a licensed medical, educational, legal or accounting professional.

Before you begin any change in your lifestyle in any way, you will consult a licensed professional to ensure that you are doing what's best for your situation.

This book provides content related to educational and financial topics. As such, use of this book implies your acceptance of this disclaimer.

TABLE OF CONTENTS

"What I think is really a big, shameful thing that higher education has been doing to students for years is selling everybody on the idea that college is a golden ticket to the middle class."

Dr Andrew Gillen
Texas Public Policy Foundation

INTRODUCTION

A Job in Sales: First Hired, Never Fired

You should be a car salesman!

I got that a lot in my twenties. When people said it, I was never sure if it was a compliment or an insult. It was likely intended as a compliment to say that I had good sales skills. But yet … Even as a kid, I was aware of the "used car salesman" jokes—that a car salesman would tell you anything under the sun to close the sale, whether it was *"If you purchase now, I'll throw in a free keyring,"* or, *"Seriously, I just sold my last one to your neighbor. He was here just the other day. Great guy."*

I get it. "I'm in sales" is not everyone's idea of a dream vocation. No one graduates from college and races home to delight their mom and dad by announcing the news that they just landed a job as a telemarketer or a car salesman. I was no different.

My first sales job was not exactly glamorous.

I sold software over the phone to cold leads who had called in from a newspaper ad. Actually, my first sales job was *getting* the sales job. I had no experience and a largely blank resume. Luckily, my older brother got hired at the firm, so my pitch to get the job was that I learned everything I knew from him. My sales pitch worked. In my first month there, I made $8,000 in commissions. Earning $8,000 in a month—and note that this was my FIRST month—was pretty big stuff in the world of a 24-year-old.

My job didn't sound glamorous, right? Not the kind of stuff that impresses as an opening line on a first date. If you say, "I'm an attorney," that sounds pretty impressive. Everyone from your parents to your friends to your family pet goes, "*Oh, wow, that's great!*"

But here's the thing, $8,000 a month was as much as most attorneys made back then. To get to that point, though, they had spent at least seven years in college and law school and had invested a quarter-million dollars or more in tuition. How much time did I have to spend in school to be able to earn $8,000 my first month? *Less than two weeks of basic sales training.*

Let's recap and summarize the first fundamental lesson I learned about sales:

- Earn $8,000 in one month as an attorney: 7+ years studying + $250,000 in tuition.

- Earn $8,000 in one month as a salesperson: 12 days of training.

If you have a highlighter pen, you may want to go ahead and highlight those two lines.

Ironically, even though I was earning more money than I had dreamed of at 24 AND loving every minute of it, I was embarrassed by my identity as a "salesman." I started crafting words to disguise what I did so it sounded more professional and impressive.

We've all seen how people do this on LinkedIn and other social media platforms.

Oh, so you're a waitress? *"No! I'm a Food & Beverage Brand Ambassador specializing in Service and Communication."*

Oh, so you're unemployed and living in your parent's basement? *"No! I'm a Netflix Specialist and the Managing Director of a Subterranean Nonprofit. I have a skill endorsement from my friend Dave, who's in the same industry."*

My best shot at dressing up my occupation was to call myself a "Client Acquisition Specialist." I thought that was pretty smart at the time. Still, it always got the same response *"Oh, so you're a salesman?"* Busted!

Well, the journey was worth all the knocks and jokes. I came to realize that being a salesman is an identity to wear with pride. Where did my knack for sales get me? Today, I own a multi-million-dollar-a-year sales company that employs more than 100 full-time salespeople. I've generated more than one billion dollars' worth of revenue for my clients. Not bad for a college dropout!

So, what's the point of that story?

2020 changed everything for everyone. The pandemic has split the world into "before" and "after." Shutdowns meant that a lot of good folks were laid off. And a lot of those good folks weren't invited back when businesses reopened.

You may be one of these good folks, or you may be living in fear of becoming one of those good folks. However, there is a group—a small group—of people in nearly every company who have no worries at all. They're safe, they're untouchable, they're the stars of the show that can't possibly go on without them.

These elite men and women were busier than ever during the crisis, continuing to do their work and continuing to earn solid incomes. These modern-day superheroes weren't worried if they would be asked back because they never left.

While others beg and plead to make a case for keeping their jobs, members of this group are doing quite the opposite. They are the ones with the upper hand. Many of them have found that they prefer the new style of working from home and many will tell their bosses that they have decided to work from home permanently. And the thing is, the bosses will happily agree because they *need* these people. They *need* their skill set.

You've probably figured out who these "people" are. That's right, they are SALESPEOPLE.

Even during the worst of the pandemic, skilled salespeople were in high demand.

When forced into a corner, companies view most employees as non-essential. When company survival is at stake, even top management is at risk. In fact, it's often the top salary earners who fall first. But no company, no matter the industry, niche, or size, can survive without sales.

Here is the one basic, immutable truth about being in business: A company IS sales. There is no company without sales. It's a simple mathematical equation: Sales = Company.

We live in uncertain times. Regardless of whether you're looking for a new career, need to pivot quickly, want to make yourself irreplaceable right where you are, or want to make sure you have the skills to keep your own business running through good times and bad, the skill of "sales" is what will get you there.

I wrote this book for YOU. I want to show you that there is a realistic, achievable way for you to increase your income. You don't have to go back to school for years on end. You don't have to work three "side gigs." You simply need to acquire the skills that will make you a professional—and highly paid—salesperson.

Then you'll know why saying "I'm in sales" is simply awesome.

CHAPTER 1

Sales: A Recession-Proof Profession

Every good sales pitch has a promise. Although I've got my author hat on, I'm always a salesman first, so I won't disappoint you. I have a very big promise for you and here it is:

Once you learn to sell *correctly and professionally*, you will never be out of work again in your life.

This isn't an empty promise to get you to buy the upgraded version with the bigger engine and fancier sound system. This is a real-world promise. You may think this promise sounds a little "too good to be true," but you'll see that it simply makes sense.

As I said in my introduction, every business on the planet needs sales. Company = Sales, or it might be more accurate to say Sales = Company. This is the truth that I learned early on in my career—whatever profession or business you are in, you can never the need to sell.

If you're a doctor, a therapist, or a surgeon, you need to get patients. If you're a lawyer, a builder, or a photographer, you need to get clients. If you're a dog walker, you need to get dogs on leashes. No doggies, no walkies, no money!

Sales is Quantifiable

Many employees do work that, while valuable, is abstract in value. That is, their work can't be quantified. Exactly what Janet does for the company in Human Resources can't be expressed in numerical terms. (By the way, this is a very useful position, I'm just using it as an example.)

But Louise in Sales? The big boss is pretty clear about what Louise in Sales does for the company. He pays her $10,000 a month, and she brings in $100,000 a month. There is no room to even consider whether Louise in Sales is a worthwhile employee. It's a mathematical certainty.

Sales is Recession-Proof

In fact, sales is not just recession-proof, it is recession-*strong*. The worse things get, the more in demand a professional salesperson becomes. Imagine you own a business and the country is entering a recession. What are the two biggest things on your mind? Your first thought is most likely, "Where can I cut costs?" and your second thought is undoubtedly, "How can I get more sales?"

In tough times these are really the only two thoughts that will go through a business owner's mind. And by the way, they can be in either order.

We also live in uncertain times because of technology. The future looks unsteady for many people, as jobs, and even entire industries, increasingly become redundant. Many employees are terrified because technology is moving so quickly. We wonder if we'll be next. Feel safe now? What about in 20 years? A lot can change at the pace we're going.

Sales is Future-Proof

Salespeople will always be needed. Yes, there have been and continue to be rapid advancements on automated and web-based sales platforms and methods, but these are all designed to *help* the salesperson, not replace them. In fact, as technology advances, so does the need for *better* salespeople.

Think about this: In the 1950s, a door-to-door salesperson would walk the local neighborhood, knock on doors and try to sell a vacuum cleaner. On a good day, they might pitch to 20 clients.

Today, technology hasn't replaced the need for a person to sell vacuum cleaners. However, with the aid of technology, instead of prospecting a local neighborhood, salespeople can now "knock on the doors" of millions of people all across the world. What does this mean? It means there will be a need for MORE skilled, professional salespeople!

Sales is Age-Proof

Sales is a skill that never gets old, that never goes out of favor. Just like riding a bicycle or mastering the first level of Super Mario Brothers, once you learn the skills right, you'll have them for life. If you want to, you can continue to work in sales well into your 70s and 80s as your retirement gig—and from the comfort of your home!

But there is this curious thing...

As I touched on in the introduction, people often don't like the idea of being identified as a "salesperson." It's a job title that unfortunately brings up negative connotations for many people. That's something that's really sad and unfortunate.

The reason for the association is that there are many completely unskilled "salespeople." There's no law against anyone sticking a badge on their chest and saying, "Now I'm a salesperson." There are no qualifications or certifications needed. When many people think of "salesperson," they think of Jimmy the Used Car Salesman, who's been using the same, tired one-liner for more than a decade and who laughs a bit too much at his own jokes. But a PROFESSIONAL salesperson, a salesperson that is highly skilled and experienced, that's as noble as a profession can get.

And there's this. Once anyone finds out how much money you make as a sales professional, well, the arguments, the snide remarks, the put-downs... *will all fade away.*

Today, every single person who comes to work for me goes through the exact same training process.

This book lays out that process.

Our salespeople make incredible amounts of money, not because they're naturally gifted at selling, but because they follow my proven system. My system has helped established sales professionals double and even triple their best-ever commission record. It's the exact process and system that allows our top earners to make $700,000 per year while working only a few hours per day.

The majority of our salespeople earn at least $75,000 per year.

Consider what that means. These are people who went to "school" for two months and then went straight to earning $75,000 a year. They genuinely have the potential to make more than $250,000 a year working just 25 to 30 hours per week.

These are real, actual everyday people. Over the years, I've watched hundreds of newbies transform into sales wizards and earn more than they've ever dreamed of.

This book lays out the roadmap of how you can do that, too.

KEY TAKEAWAYS

➢ Once you learn to sell correctly and professionally, you will never be out of work again in your life.

➢ Sales = Company / Company = Sales. Every company in the world needs to sell.

Benefits of a Profession in Sales:

➢ Quantifiable value.

➢ Recession-proof.

➢ Future-proof.

➢ Age-proof.

CHAPTER 2

By the Numbers:
The Case for a Career in Sales

There are many reasons why a career in sales makes a lot of good, sound sense. If you consider the time and costs involved in getting a college degree compared to learning professional sales techniques, and then look at the income potential and lifestyle of being in sales, the numbers speak for themselves.

Most people equate having a four-year degree with a step-up in earning power. Of course, we know that's not necessarily the case these days. Plus, getting a degree usually takes more than four years. In the average, non-flagship public university, only 19% of students graduate on time. Even at flagship research public universities, the on-time graduation rate is only 36%. Only 50 of the more than 580 public four-year institutions have on-time graduation rates above 50%.

On average, today's students take more than two years to earn an associate degree. The numbers show that it's more like 3.3 academic years. Bachelor's degree earners take more than four years to finish. The average is 5.1 academic years. But those stats are for someone who starts college right out of high school. If you are under 30, it takes five years to get a bachelor's degree. However, if you're over 30, that same degree could take you THIRTEEN YEARS. Why is that? Well, at that age, you usually have a full-time job plus family obligations, and you only have the time to take one class a semester—maybe two if you don't want a life.

Now, let's dive into the income numbers and make a case for SALES.

The average income of a person with a high school diploma is $37,000 a year. If you have a bachelor's degree, it's $46,000 a year, a difference of $9,000 a year. Getting a bachelor's degree at a public four-year college (if you're an in-state student) will cost you $60,000, on average. That figure is on the very low end of today's college costs. Considering the salary bump you'll get from having a college degree, it will take you nearly seven years to break even compared to the salary you'd have with just a high school diploma. So from the time you start college until the time you are able to "break even" it will be nearly eleven years.

If you look at it from this perspective, it's a pretty crazy route!

The average time it will take you to learn professional selling techniques is 12 weeks. Yes, you can complete sales training in just three months! You could possibly learn these techniques in four weeks, but to really study and understand and absorb, it will take you about three months of hard study, hard practice, and finally, success. Learn the skill of selling, and in 8 to 12 WEEKS, you can be in a position to make back your investment in training in four months.

Let's take it a step further. Let's compare the highest-earning careers—doctors—with the earning potential of a professional sales career.

To become a medical doctor, getting the required degrees plus residency can take you about 12 years—more than that for some specialties. And while medical professionals do make good money—the ten highest-earning careers in America are all in medical fields—these folks work insane hours and have practically no personal life.

Yes, earnings for these professionals, from dentist to anesthesiologist, are impressive, with average incomes ranging from $174,000 to $265,000. At the same time, their stress levels are far beyond anything you or I might experience. They can face life-or-death decisions on a daily basis, and let's not even mention the annual malpractice insurance premiums, which are more than what I paid for my last new car.

Now, let's look at the experience of someone who becomes a professional salesperson compared to the experience of someone who becomes a medical doctor:

- Saves hundreds of thousands of dollars in tuition.

- Ready to start earning income within three months.

- Gets to a decent, professional level of income within two years.

- Works no more than 40 hours a week, maybe 45 if they are really pushing it.

Think about these numbers: After working for two years as a professional salesperson, you have about a real chance of earning an income of EXACTLY what medical professionals earn. Imagine that. All the money, but with the time off and peace of mind to be able to spend the money and time with your family. And even if you don't quite hit that income mark, your life could still be much better off than theirs.

Let's close with the following numbers. Many, many—I would venture to say a very decent percentage of professional salespeople in the United States—earn MORE than $174,000 a year. I mentioned earlier that my top salesperson makes more than $700,000 a year. Other salespeople work for me who earn more than $250,000 a year. You can realistically aim for this level of income as a sales pro.

KEY TAKEAWAYS

- The route to becoming a professional salesperson makes great sense in terms of cost and time versus obtaining a college degree.

- A college degree realistically takes more than four years to obtain and even up to thirteen years if you attend part-time.

- Even with the increase in earning potential from having a college degree, it can take you six years or more to settle your college loan debt.

- The course of study to become a professional salesperson takes just three months.

- The cost of a sales course can be paid back within just four months.

Benefits of Sales Training

- Start earning income within three months.

- Get to a professional level of income within two years.

- Work no more than 40 hours a week.

- Practically unlimited earning potential. Many professional salespeople earn as much or more than medical doctors!

ACTION STEP

Here's your first "sales" assignment! Ask a family member, a friend, a colleague—someone that you respect—if you can talk through your thoughts about pursuing a career in sales. Use this chapter's points as part of your "sales pitch." Listen to the feedback from your "client" and see if you can "persuade" them that this all makes sense when you say it out loud.

CHAPTER 3

Use a Bigger Shovel

Greatest Potential is in 100% Commission Positions

Let me set the scene. It was a hot summer day, and I was on vacation with my family at the beach in Oceanside, California. Everything was perfect as we surfed and skim boarded and played in the sand. My youngest child had an idea that he thought was the best idea of all time. He wanted to dig a hole in the sand so big that we could all fit in it. Fair enough, that is a pretty cool idea.

We got to work and tried to dig our Super Hole before the tide came in. The only tools we had were little plastic sandbox shovels, so we could scoop out about four little cups of sand at a time. In short order, I realized that our seemingly innocent project was probably going to take all day! I thought to myself, if only I had a bigger shovel, I could dig this hole in no time and get back to my surfing!

While this is a short story and maybe not as dramatic as I made it out to be, it does have a HUGE moral.

The moral to the story is this: If you are going to make the effort to sell, you might as well move the most amount of 'sand' as you can with each scoop! It takes just as much effort to sell something for $500 as it does to sell something for $5,000. If you want to make a ton of money, why not sell things that cost $5,000 or more? That's Big Shovel thinking!

When most people start out in sales, they begin by playing with little shovels. Little shovels are jobs where you take a salary plus commission. To the beginner, this feels like a 'safe' route. Having a salary makes you feel like you have a 'real' job and that you won't starve. But that feeling of safety comes at a price, which is that no matter how hard you work, your income is going to be small. In effect, your employer is saying to you, "Guess what! Every month you're going to be using the same little shovel!" It may feel safe to have the security of a salary, but there's only so much you can fit in a little shovel.

Here are some examples of 'Little Shovel' salary plus commission jobs:

- Inbound call center, selling low-ticket items. These are products or services that retail for less than $500. Making 5% commission means that at most, you're earning $25 per sale.

- Pest control sales. This is a tougher job as it's likely to be an 'outbound' situation where you are contacting people cold, either on the phone or by walking the neighborhood. An average sale may be $600, and you're likely to earn around $60 a sale.

- Jewelry store. You'll get 5% of each sale you make. That's great if you can sell a $5,000 diamond ring every day, but in reality, you'll need to gain at least 6 to 12 months of experience before being allowed to handle the larger sales.

- Car dealership. Typically at a car dealership, you are given a choice between a guaranteed salary per month or a large commission without the safety net of a salary. Most car salespeople starting out will go for the first option, worried that they don't have leads or experience.

All those jobs are perfectly respectable places to start. But right from the beginning, you need to keep your eye on getting that shiny Big Shovel. You need to find big-ticket items to sell that pay big-ticket commissions.

The only place you will find sales jobs that pay high commissions on high-ticket items are sales jobs that are 100% commission only, no salary. To achieve success, you'll need to take off your "training wheels," and the sooner, the better. Most people panic when they hear 'commission only,' and they start to imagine themselves starving and out on the street. It may sound like too much of a risk, too high a gamble.

But then consider this: To become a doctor, a chiropractor, or a dentist, you'll need to spend at least eight years in school and go into debt to the tune of several hundred thousand dollars. Once you're finally a full-fledged medical professional, you might want to set up your own office, and guess what? You'll be working for 100% commission! There's no safety net of an employer giving you a basic salary. You'll only earn when you get patients.

How to Spot a Big Shovel

What does a Big Shovel look like? Generally, a Big Shovel is any sale over $3,000. The higher the price point, the lower the commission, but the rule of thumb is that you should be getting 10% to 15% commission on anything over $3,000. So, if you're selling a $4,500 machine, then you should be earning a commission of $450 to $675.

So, where are the Big Shovel jobs hiding? Here are just a few jobs that offer high commissions on high-ticket sales:

- Real estate.

- Insurance.

- Education programs.

- Non-accredited certificate programs.

- Cybersecurity certificates.

- Medical equipment.

- Pharmaceuticals.

- Security systems.

Consider these benefits of working on commission when you sell higher ticket items:

- You earn more money on each sale.

- You save on taxes because, as a commissioned sales-person, you can claim business expense deductions at tax time.

- You are in full control of your work, effort, time spent, and schedule—you can set your own goals and work when you want.

The Ultimate Shovel: High Commission + Recession Resistant Industry

The best scenario of all is to find a job selling high-ticket items that are also recession-proof. That way, you'll always have work and an income (a potentially high income, by the way) regardless of whether the economy is up, down, or sideways.

These are the industries that still typically thrive during a downturn in the economy:

- Medical equipment

- Pharmaceuticals

- Education-Based Degree or Certificate programs

- Insurance

Real estate is a high-ticket, high-commission example of a Big Shovel, but be warned it is NOT recession-proof. In fact, real estate is one of the hardest-hit industries in a recession. The real estate industry rides the waves; it will always go through ups and downs. When the economy is booming, and interest rates are playing along, there's plenty of high-fiving to do. But when things go bad, and they always do at some point, real estate agents can suffer greatly. Only too recently, we saw an example of the devastating effects on the real estate market caused by the dramatic market crash in 2008.

So now that we've looked at 'shovels' and their sizes, I hope I've convinced you that you need to seek out the big ones. In addition to size, you need to seek out those businesses and industries that are more recession-proof.

Now that I've made my pitch on why sales is such an awesome career choice, turn to the next chapter to begin your training to become a sales professional.

KEY TAKEAWAYS

➢ Use "Big Shovel" thinking—use the same time and effort to sell bigger ticket items.

➢ Avoid the perceived "safety" of salaried jobs. Work for 100% commission and you will be rewarded with a higher income.

Working on commission selling higher-ticket items means:

➢ More money earned on each sale.

➢ Tax savings.

➢ Full control over your own schedule.

ACTION STEP

Make a list of all the high-ticket sales niches that you can think of and take note of which ones appeal to you the most.

CHAPTER 4

You Better Take It Personally

The worst piece of sales advice I've ever heard—and it's depressingly common—is that "a salesperson should disconnect from the result." The trainer who offered this advice was attempting to teach people how to deal with customer rejection.

It seems like sensible advice at first—if, as a salesperson, you are not connected emotionally, then you won't feel down and rejected when a client doesn't buy. The trainer followed up his first bit of bad advice with an equally incorrect statement: "Don't worry, they are not saying no to you, they are saying no to the product."

That's about as true as when you're dumped by your boyfriend/girlfriend, and they say, "It's not about you." I'm afraid it very much is about you! Skillful selling is 100% *personal.*

Your customer is buying *you.* Always remember that. Most sales are made because of how you made your customer *feel.*

The most effective and powerful tool in the salesperson's tool kit is **mindset**. Sales is the transfer of energy. The transfer of enthusiasm. The transfer of confidence. And that transfer takes place between you, as the salesperson, and your customer. That transfer makes things personal.

Your job is to get your customer to like you, enjoy talking to you, trust you, and ultimately let you guide them into making a decision. Each sales pitch is a unique human interaction. For a successful transfer to take place, your energy needs to come from a genuine and authentic place.

As human beings, we have acute natural instincts for spotting authenticity (or the opposite!). Your customer will know if you are sharing a genuine, personal transfer of energy or if you are rotely reading the same sales script for the 100th time.

Here are the *Four Golden Rules of Sales*. Learn them, memorize them, repeat them to the family pet if you have to, and most of all, incorporate them into your daily life as a sales professional.

Golden Rule 1: You must be a better person before you can be a better salesperson.

Golden Rule 2: Get your mind right, because the customer's is rarely right.

Golden Rule 3: Selling is the transfer of enthusiasm and buying confidence.

Golden Rule 4: You can't give what you don't have. Get your enthusiasm and confidence up to a 12 on a 10-point scale.

On any sales team made up of more than ten people, everyone in the team will have the same lead quality and the same volume of leads. They will have the same training, the same management systems. They will have the same teacher and sales manager, and they're repping the exact same product.

But inevitably, there will be top, middle, and bottom performers. With all things being seemingly equal, what is the ingredient that makes for the difference in performance?

I'll tell you a personal story where I learned one of my most important sales lessons. If you recall, my first sales job was selling software over the phone, and I worked in the same office as my older brother.

Still fairly new to sales, I was on the phone with a potential customer, and they were asking, what I felt, were antagonizing questions, skeptical questions such as "What about this? What about that?" I was feeling irritated, and my tone of voice became increasingly defensive.

Out of the blue, my brother leaned over my shoulder and pressed his finger down on the phone's hold button. "You sound like a jerk," he said matter-of-factly. I snapped back at him, saying that I didn't know what he was talking about. He didn't say anything else, just looked at me, and I quickly realized he was 100% right.

Embarrassed, I got off mute and took control of the conversation, first by being genuine with the client. I said, "You know what? You've got some very valid points, some very legitimate questions, I think we need to discuss. I've been a little defensive. Let's take a step back. Let's address each of your questions and see if we can find out if this is a good fit for you."

This radically changed the entire conversation, and I ended up closing the sale for a very nice commission. The lesson I learned was that *I needed to change who I was, not try to change who the client was.*

Let's identify a few things you CAN change so that people will want to buy from you. These are things that you can control to increase the buying confidence of a customer on the phone.

Don't be late. If you're late for an appointment, you are, in essence, saying to the customer, "You're not as important as the person I was just speaking to."

Speak with confidence. Master your diction, enunciate your words clearly, ask simple, succinct questions. Nothing creates a feeling of trust as much as the way you speak.

Use your customer's name. Make sure you have your customer's name up on your screen at all times. And make sure to use their name as often as possible. People love to hear their own name. People also love to have a chance to talk about themselves.

THE POWER OF MOOD

People can immediately and instinctively pick up on the kind of mood you're in, even if you're on a phone call. In fact, they may even be able to pick up on your mood through your email! Tony Robbins, the celebrated life and business strategist and coach, explains that your physiology and your emotions cannot oppose each other: "Your physiology, the way your body moves, the way your body is, cannot oppose, in other words, be opposite of your emotions."

Here's a little exercise for you to try to see how this works.

Slump your shoulders, make a frown, and look down at the ground. Try and say as excitedly as possible, "Hi there! I've got the most amazing product to show you; it will change your life!" You'll see that you simply can't get your voice to sound convincingly excited. Your voice will be guided by your shriveled physical state.

Now try the opposite. Sit up straight, raise your eyebrows, put a big smile on your face, and raise your hands up. Now say, "I'm terribly depressed today, everything is going wrong, and I'm not coping." Sounds a bit silly saying those words, right?

The mood of a conversation can mean the difference between closing a sale and adding a big fat zero to your bank account. Just as your physicality dictates the quality of your voice, the mood you set dictates the mood of your call. Mood is infectious. If your voice is bright, cheerful, and upbeat, chances are the person you are talking to will mirror you. In the same way that it feels unnatural to sound sad when you're smiling, it feels unnatural to them to sound negative when you're upbeat.

THE ZONE

In the field of psychology, there is a theory known as "The Zone of Proximal Development." Its description is this: "Most people live and operate inside of this zone of proximal development. Under their power, under their own will, they can bump into the walls of this zone, but they generally will not go outside it. The greatest amount of learning and the greatest amount of opportunity in growth in life is when you are outside that zone, when you're outside the zone of proximal development."

Yeah, that's a bit of a wordy and confusing definition that needs to be read a few times, but here is what it boils down to: this "zone" is a "safe zone." The average person who ends up buying what you are selling will start off thinking "no." It's a habit. Saying no means they don't have to think terribly hard. They don't have to make the effort of taking out their credit card and reading you the number. They don't have to commit.

Most people need to go through a process of being persuaded. If people naturally made decisions and took action when presented with a solution to their needs, we would not need salespeople. We'd simply throw up some advertisements and sit back. But that is not the case. This is why salespeople are vital and also why they—that is, YOU—will always be needed.

There are many facets to being a skilled salesperson. You've got to be part therapist, part salesperson, part entertainer, part friend, and part antagonist. It takes a balance of all these roles to coax someone out of their Zone of Proximal Development. Your job is to gently guide the customer and make them feel safe and positive so they can step outside the walls of their safe zone.

The other day, someone asked me what I did for a living. I said, "I'm a therapist, salesperson, entertainer, and friend." They looked at me funny. But it's true!

Getting someone out of their safety zone and turning a "no" into a "yes!" is part skill and part art form. It's not about arm-twisting or bullying someone into making a decision. Some unskilled salespeople try to use an aggressive selling tactic to force a customer into saying yes. This is a bad idea and will only turn a "no" into a "NO!"

I sometimes like to think of the process like dating. Think about how you would act on a first date. You wouldn't be aggressive and demand that your date agree to be your girlfriend/boyfriend. You'd entertain them, tell stories, ask questions, make them feel special and heard, and generally show your best side.

The dance of the date is to persuade the person sitting across the candle-lit table to feel comfortable and excited to step out of their Zone of Proximal Development.

These are some of the most important concepts in getting to a "yes." "Yes" is your goal. I have a sticky note on the side of my computer monitor. On it, I've written the word "YES." The more people who say "yes" to you, the more incredible your life as a salesperson becomes.

KEY TAKEAWAYS

- ➢ Skillful selling is 100% personal.

- ➢ Most sales are made by how you make the customer feel.

- ➢ Sales is a transfer of energy and enthusiasm.

- ➢ Your energy needs to come from an authentic place.

The Four Golden Rules of Sales

- ➢ Golden Rule 1: You must be a better person before you can be a better salesperson.

- ➢ Golden Rule 2: Get your mind right, because the customer's is rarely right.

- ➢ Golden Rule 3: Sales is the transfer of enthusiasm and buying confidence.

- ➢ Golden Rule 4: You can't give what you don't have.

Three things you can do to increase buying confidence:

➢ Don't be late.

➢ Speak with confidence.

➢ Use your customer's name.

Remember these concepts:

➢ *Customers can instinctively sense your mood. Your mood is directly influenced by your physical posture.*

➢ Most customers are stuck within "The Zone of Proximal Development"—a zone of safety where they default to a "no" position to avoid effort.

➢ Your job as a salesperson is to guide your client outside of this zone and help them feel comfortable and excited to go from a "no" to a "yes!"

ACTION STEPS

Experiment with different physical positions and postures while saying out loud as positively and enthusiastically as possible: "Hi, this is [first name], I'm really glad to be speaking with you!" Try this in a slumped position and then try this sitting upright with your chest pushed out. Record yourself on your phone and notice how you can easily "hear" the difference your posture makes!

CHAPTER 5

Empathy and Ego

Harvard University did a fascinating study. This seven-year study looked at what makes good salespeople... *good salespeople.*

The study was undertaken to examine a problem in the insurance industry that existed for more than three decades. The problem was attrition. The industry would continually need to hire a mass number of salespeople to combat attrition. Companies would spend millions and millions of dollars on hiring insurance salespeople and bringing them on board, only to see most of them leave within two years.

In year one in insurance sales, companies would see a 50% attrition rate. *50% of the people they hired would drop out within one year.* In year two, the attrition would hit 80%. The insurance industry had an obvious problem, and it was at a loss to explain it. Collectively, companies spent a massive amount of effort, time, and money on recruiting, and nearly all that investment would slip away within two years.

Over the course of 35 years, they studied the problem, increased base salaries, instituted and increased bonuses, and more. Companies added training and information to help the sales reps. They started inundating their sales force with as much as they possibly could to make their sales jobs that much better.

But, for 35 years, the attrition rate stubbornly remained at 50% in year one. By year three, it was still 80%. 35 years of incentives. 35 years of effort. 35 years of spending millions and millions of dollars did not change the statistic one bit. 50% attrition in year one.

Harvard looked at this problem and decided to conduct a research study to try to get to the bottom of what was going on. It did a seven-year study on what makes a good salesperson, trying to find factors that would predict success. The study's findings were published in the Harvard Business Review in 2006. The reason why I like this article so much is that its conclusions are in perfect alignment with what I've taught and what I believe, and what I have implemented for myself in my sales career.

A common theme in this book is, "I can give two people the same script, and they will get two different results." I also teach that if you can change a person, if you can change who a person is for the better, you will change their results as a salesperson. I believe sales is tremendously impacted by your psychology, who you are as a person. These beliefs of mine have come from experience, but I was delighted to come across this study as it validated my approach.

After seven years of study, Harvard concluded the two key components that made for successful salespeople were **Empathy** and **Ego.**

EMPATHY

Oftentimes, you will see people talk about empathy as a synonym of sympathy. And that's not exactly true.

Empathy is your ability to understand how somebody else feels.

If you have empathy, you understand where your customer is coming from, you understand what it feels like to be them. Sympathy is where you *share* the feeling that somebody else has. In other words, if somebody is mourning, an empathetic person can understand it, and they can show kindness, and they can reflect it, and they can understand it. A sympathetic person will actually take on the feeling of mourning. And now you both are experiencing it. So, there is a difference. There's a subtle difference between empathy and sympathy.

The seven-year study from Harvard found that the top salespeople in the world have empathy. They have an uncanny ability to understand the emotions of other people, what other people are feeling. Think back to the last five to ten times you've interacted with a salesperson. You'll probably not be able to put your finger on why some of these experiences stood out, but then you realize, "The sales experiences that I had as a customer, the ones where I felt like somebody was listening to me, they understood me, were a way better experience than the ones where they were just trying to make a commission, the ones where they were just trying to plow through, the ones that didn't really listen to what I said, they didn't really care what I said."

As a salesperson, your empathy will have a huge impact on your ability to sell. You must be able to connect on an emotional level with another human being without actually taking on their feelings.

If you flip from *understanding* somebody's situation to *feeling* their situation, you're on a very slippery slope, and you'll end up being in a place that we call *commiserating*. When you both are feeling down, your effectiveness as a salesperson plummets. In the empathetic scenario, if you can understand where somebody's at, you can understand their feelings, you've listened to them, you comprehend what they're feeling, but you can maintain the emotion and the positive energy you need to influence them, you'll be a successful salesperson. You want to maintain and exhibit your empathy without switching over into sympathy, which could easily slide into commiserating.

Commiserating sounds like this. A customer says, "You know, Ryan, things have just been really, really bad lately. I just really don't understand how I can get out of this. I lost my job, things have been really dark, I can't even see the light at the end of the tunnel." A sympathetic salesperson might take on the same mood, saying, "Aw, I know what you mean. Man, five years ago, I went through the exact same thing, and I just ... man, when you get down in the dumps like that, I know. I feel the same way sometimes." That is commiserating. That brings your energy down to their energy level, which is NOT something you want to do.

An empathetic person would have a conversation like this. Your customer, John, says to you, "Ryan, things are really bad. I lost my job; I really can't see the light at the end of the tunnel." As an empathetic salesperson, I could say, "John, I can understand exactly what you're saying, and I can imagine that that might be a tough place for you to be in. But can I tell you, with that in mind, I just have to congratulate you for still making the effort. John, you're on a call right now that could possibly change your life. John, I believe I have some information that I could share with you that could put you in a position where you could reverse everything you just said."

So what happened here? I understood why he was feeling the way he was, but I didn't take on his emotions. Sometimes we think that to make an emotional connection, we need to become a customer's friend. That's a big mistake! We'll take a closer look at this, but always remember—the easiest person to ever say no to is your friend.

EGO

The second thing that the Harvard team identified as a common trait among good salespeople is a really interesting one. It's their *ego*.

This sounds kind of crazy at first—on the face of it, these findings seem to be polar opposites! If you look at the etymology of empathy—understanding somebody's emotions—and then you look at the definition and the origin and the etymology of ego, from the Latin word ego, it actually means I. Myself. Ego. Me. But nevertheless, the Harvard study found that a successful salesperson has a healthy amount of ego.

If you think about it, ego has to do with self-identification. It has to do with self-accomplishment. It has to do with self-esteem, your inner strength. Oftentimes, ego exhibits itself as confidence. Ego, as we typically think about it, has a negative connotation. Rarely does somebody compliment you on your ego. More likely, they would criticize you for having a 'big' ego.

According to the Harvard study, the most successful salespeople have an incredible balance between their empathy and ego. Here's how the article described the balance: A salesperson who has too much empathy will connect on an emotional level with somebody, and they will never close them. Somebody who has too much empathy is going to become their friend, and that customer won't buy from their friend. They will say no to their friend, they'll ghost their friend, and then later on, they'll come back and buy from the company from somebody else who wasn't a total pushover.

So, with too much empathy, you will not be a good closer.

On the other hand, a person who has too much ego is going to bulldoze people for their own benefit and only try to close them so they can make a commission. If you exhibit too much empathy or ego, you're going to struggle in a sales capacity. If you can find a place of balance between the two, meaning you can connect with customers on an emotional level, but you still stay firm on your self-interest of succeeding, closing, doing your job, and making it happen, if you can combine those two in a healthy balance, you are going to be an excellent salesperson.

One of the greatest and most common compliments that I get in my role as a sales rep, or as the owner of a company, or when I get to speak on stage, is, "Ryan, I love to listen to you speak because you sound so real. You just sound like a real person." And to me, that translates into me having an ability to connect with people on an emotional level and have empathy with them, but I also have a strong enough ego to where I can connect with them and push them to make buying decisions.

So always find a way to balance your empathy and ego.

When you are on the phone with somebody, when you are trying to sell them something, you can't just be emotional the whole time; you'll never close them. At the same time, you can't push a friend outside their Zone of Proximal Development. You have to have that ego pop in a little bit. You have to have that strength and that self-confidence, that inner drive, that inner fire that says, "No, I'm going to hit my goals." The ego in a salesperson says, "I'm going to hit my goals." The ego in a salesperson says, "I'm going to be number one. If my goal is to convert 10% of my leads, I won't sleep until I do it." That's the ego-driven side of a salesperson.

The empathy side of a salesperson says, "Man, I get to do my job, connect with people, and help people change their lives. This is awesome." When you're interacting with a customer, you need to know when it's time to turn on the empathy and when it's time to turn on the ego. The healthy relationship and the healthy balance between the two are going to make you an incredible salesperson.

SAME SCRIPT, DIFFERENT RESULTS

Let's back up a few steps and go back to my first sales observation. I can give two people the same script, and I will get two different results. I can tell you that two salespeople can be given the same opportunity and deliver very different results. They can be given the same script, the same product description, the same attention, the same training, the same resources. And one will set themselves apart.

Where does this difference come from? It's my belief that if you can balance your ego and your empathy, you are going to be somebody that people want to talk to. You're going to be their companion on the one hand and their coach on the other hand. They're not going to say no to you because they know that you understand and you have higher expectations for them.

The ego inside of you will project your own expectations of yourself, and you'll project it onto them. When you want to be number one on your sales team, you will project that onto your customer. And they will want to be number one in their category of life. The empathy side of you is going to spend most of its time in the beginning of your conversation. Your discovery process is going to be mostly about empathy. Listening, connecting. And you absolutely do not want to fake or manufacture this. Be a human. Be real. Listen to them. Everyone has a unique circumstance.

I was taking some calls for a client recently, just to do some split testing, and I happened to get on the phone with a guy from Africa. He had recently moved to the States and was struggling to get a job. His visa status was a complex obstacle, and he couldn't speak English all that well. He didn't really have a lot of technical background, internet background, anything like that. Now, it would have been very easy for me to just disconnect from the call and not have any empathy towards this man at all. But as he told me his story, I started thinking to myself, "Man, what kind of gumption does this guy have? What drives somebody to move to a different country where you can't get a job, to pick up the phone and try to find a way to start your own business? What gets into this man? What does he have that gives him that level of belief?"

So, I started asking more and more questions. And the more questions I asked, the more I related to him. I realized that I had that same kind of drive. His father owned a t-shirt company in Africa, selling t-shirts online. We started talking about that, and some of the stuff he had done was in perfect alignment with what I had done in my past. Pretty soon, talking to this African man that didn't speak English as his first language, living in the United States, on the phone coming from a completely different world than mine, we found a commonality. We built a relationship of trust through listening and empathizing about where each other had come from.

Once we made that connection, and once he could hear that in my voice, then I could go through a sales process with him that would compel him to take action. I could guide him down that path, and it turned out to be a fantastic phone call.

I recently got an email from one of our reps asking me for help with a situation. It's interesting because their question was one that I get a lot. Here's what they asked: "Ryan, what would you do if someone is very standoffish and they won't give you the information you're looking for?" In other words, what would you do if you're asking all the right questions and they're holding back? The actual conversation that he had had was along the lines of, "Well, what do you want out of this program?" And they said, "That's none of your business."

Now, I want you to consider something that is very important.

I want you to live your life in a consistent and congruent way in every aspect. I want you to live your sales life the same way you would live your personal life. In other words, I want you to have the same boundaries, rules, and expectations in your sales life as you would in your personal life. Consider the following. Let's say you invite somebody over for dinner, someone new in your neighborhood, in your building, or in your workspace. You want to get to know them, so you invite them to your home for dinner. And John walks into your house, and he says, "I don't like the way you decorated this." You say, "Would you please take your shoes off?" And John says, "No, I'm not going to take my shoes off. What kind of question is that?" You sit down at dinner, and you say, "Hey, we'd like to say Grace." And John says, "No, I'm not going to say Grace." My point is this: Imagine that you invite somebody into your home. You have rules, boundaries, and expectations of how things go in your home. When you encounter a situation as with John, are you just going to ditch your rules and expectations? "Oh. Okay. Wear your dirty shoes all over my fresh white carpet. Oh. You don't like the way I decorated? Oh, maybe I'll redo my home." No. This is *your* space, *your* home. These are *your* rules. Most people agree with that.

The reason why I tell that story is I want you to think about a customer calling in as a dinner invitation. They are coming into *your* space. You create the boundaries; you create the rules. This is your call. This is the I; this is the ego. This is your call, not their call. They do not know about your program; they don't know how the process works. They have been invited into your space. And when they get in your space, you control it.

If somebody ever says to you on a sales call, "That's none of your business," you should come back empathetically and say, "John, actually, it is *exactly* my business. And here's why. I'm here to help you. And I can't help you unless I understand you. If you don't like the question, I can respect that. I can ask it differently. But at some point today, in order for me to help you properly, we're going to have to really find out how this is going to work for you, and I'm going to have to ask you some tough questions. If that's agreeable to you, we can move forward. And if it's not, we may be at an impasse, and we may just have to separate. Is that fair enough, John?"

If John is not okay with your rules, if he's not okay with your boundaries, you need to end that call. Because I promise you sometime during that call, he is not going to participate according to your rules and not going to participate according to your boundaries, and he will not buy from you. You must have the ego, and you must have the strength of character to say, "This is my home. These are the rules, this is how it works. And if you don't want to take your shoes off, you're welcome to leave."

Now, you won't do this rudely because you have empathy. You will do it with a very high level of professionalism. You'll do it with a very high level of compassion. But you can have empathy and compassion and be strong as nails at the same time. Those things don't conflict with each other. They actually support each other. Being a total jerk is when you say, "Oh, none of my business, huh? Well, I'll tell you what's none of your business, what we do. Have a great day, John," and hang up. That's uncool, that's uncalled for, that's unprofessional. As the saying goes, all you're doing then is wrestling with pigs. And when you wrestle with pigs, guess what, you both get covered in mud, and the pigs love it. Don't go that route. Always take the high road.

If somebody doesn't want to follow your rules, you come back with empathy and ego, and you say, "John, thank you for being so open with me and sharing that with me. I'm not quite sure what you expected today, but I really do need you to understand this one point. We can't move forward until I understand what it is you need. I'm here to help, and I basically hold the keys to this kingdom. I would love to help you, but I do have to ask you some tough questions. In fact, I'm going to ask you some personal questions, and some of them you probably haven't asked of yourself. And if that makes you uncomfortable, I can understand that. Maybe we'll ease into it a little bit. But I really am going to have to ask you some tough questions. If that's agreeable to you, I'd love to move forward. And if it's not, we may be at an impasse, and we just may have to shake hands and part as friends. Is that fair enough?"

If John's ego is really off the charts, he's going to hang up on you. If John's empathy is up high enough, he's going to back off, and he's going to go, "Oh. You know what? You're right. Thank you for that. I apologize. Go ahead and ask me the question." "Thanks, John, I appreciate that. Now, what exactly do you expect or want to get out of this program? I want to make sure that that's in alignment with what we think we can deliver." And then you move forward.

So, the answer to the question, "How do you deal with people that will hold back information and refuse to answer your questions?" is that those aren't the rules. You set the rules. You set the boundaries. And if they don't want to play, get off the phone. Go talk to somebody who wants to buy. That person doesn't want to buy, they want to kick tires, they want to argue, they want to piss you off. Don't wrestle with pigs. You'll both get muddy.

Sometimes we need permission to have that congruency between our personal life and our business life. If you're a good human in your business life, and you know how to set boundaries, and you're really good with managing your own time and managing expectations of people around you, you should be the exact same way in your sales life. And I'm giving you permission to do both. And if you're not good in one, but are better in the other, then practice being good in both. And I think that'll give you a really good basis to be the really good salesperson you want to be.

So let's review the two principal qualities that make for a great salesperson. Those are empathy and ego, and the healthy balance and relationship between them. That is caring about and understanding someone's emotions while at the same time caring about yourself enough to have clear standards of performance and really accomplishing what you set out to. A salesperson who has too much empathy will never close the door behind them. They can't make sales because they're just making friends. The person with too much ego is going to try to bulldoze people into submission, and everybody's going to hate them, and nobody's going to want to buy from them. They're going to write bad reviews about them.

A person who can understand somebody's state of mind and then push them toward achievement is going to win, and they're going to win more often than anybody else.

KEY TAKEAWAYS

➢ To be a good salesperson, you need to have a healthy balance of EMPATHY and EGO.

➢ Unlike empathy, sympathy will lead to commiseration and a sense of friendship, which will work against your sales goals.

➢ A customer will find it easy to say no to a friend.

➢ A healthy ego will help you drive your sales mission and close a deal.

➢ A sales call is YOUR call, so it's YOUR rules. If someone doesn't want to play by your rules, then end the call.

CHAPTER 6

Words Matter

How to Change Peoples' Lives with the Words You Say

What you say matters just as much as how you say it.

In medical school, you learn the science and physiology of how the human body works. You become a master of knowledge about the human body. In law school, you learn the ins and outs of the law. You become a master at knowing the laws and how to apply them for your clients. What do you learn in sales school? Communication! You become a master at using words to impact the way people make decisions.

In the movie *Boiler Room* (2000), which is, by the way, a story about a sales gig you do not want to be involved in, there is one line that really stood out for me: *"There is always a sale being made. Either they are selling you on why they can't, or you are selling them on why they should."*

The point is that you AND your prospective customer are making a sales pitch simultaneously. They're pitching why they can't, and you're pitching why they can and should. The best pitch wins.

HOW YOU SAY IT

"It's not what you say, but how you say it."

I'm sure you've heard this line before. Chances are, at some point, you've heard it from your significant other.

We're going to delve deeper into the "what you say," but first, let's take a look at "how you say it."

If you listen to anything from Tony Robbins or any other practitioner who uses neuro-linguistic programming (NLP), they'll often use the term "transformational vocabulary." The idea is that the words you choose to describe something can create the meaning and the intensity of what you are saying. I like to call this "Influential Language Patterns."

Let's take a look at what is probably the most common (and benign) question of all: "How are you doing today?"

Which of these replies will have the greatest impact or the greatest influence on how you receive the answer?

- Good.

- Fine.

- Fantastic.

Bet you chose C, right? They're all essentially the same answer, but why does "fantastic" have a greater impact? The answer might not be what you expect.

A and B are one-syllable words, while C is a three-syllable word. Using a multi-syllable word is an Influential Language Pattern hack. Short words indicate that you don't want to continue the subject. Using longer words shows that you are engaged, putting in the effort, and want to continue talking.

This may sound like such a small, trivial thing, but it's surprisingly powerful. Give it some thought. Imagine you get home from the office, and you ask your partner, "How was your day?" If they say "Fine," how does that make you feel? You'll instantly sense that they don't want to have a conversation about it.

Now imagine your partner saying, "Fantastic." You'll feel that they want to talk more about it, right? As you can see, the subtle difference between the length of a word really transforms the direction of the conversation.

How you say things can also include how you *ask* things. The question in the example above is actually a bad question. "How was your day?" will typically get a short answer such as "Good," "Busy," or "Crazy." The way this question is worded tells the other person that you're looking for a one-word answer.

If you want somebody to actually tell you how their day was, if you want to actually flow into a conversation, change the question. "Tell me about your day?" is a similar question, but it's really quite different. A one-word answer is not an appropriate answer to that question—and would actually be quite difficult to do! Rather, it demands a response of at least a sentence or two from the other person.

Think about someone asking you, "How was your day?" It doesn't make you feel like they really want to know, right? It's more like a standard opening line, and in return, you give a routine answer. It's not an honest transaction. But now, imagine someone says, "Tell me about your day?" That feels like a genuine question, doesn't it? The way that question is phrased shows a real interest and a desire to have a continued conversation.

WHAT YOU SAY

Being a skilled salesperson is all about knowing what to say. This is really your core skill, and my aim is to condition you into being a **Master of What to Say**. What you say can either elevate or sabotage the conversation.

The Apology

Let's take a look at the situation where an apology is needed. In this example, you arrive late to a meeting with a customer. Of course, you need to say something that acknowledges you are late, but you do NOT want to apologize. An apology immediately lowers the energy level and saying something such as "I'm sorry" focuses the attention on yourself.

Here's a way to turn it around by changing your approach. You could say something like, "John, thank you for your patience while I was wrapping up that other call. Let's go ahead and get started." You did not ignore the fact you were late, but rather than making it a lower-energy apology, you took confident control of the situation and brought the energy up by paying a compliment.

Instead of making yourself smaller, you made your client feel bigger by turning an apology into a compliment. Instead of "I'm sorry," you've told the client, "You were patient." And everyone loves a compliment. As an added bonus, you started the sentence with their name, and this tells them "the focus is all about them."

Commiserating

You'll sometimes find yourself in a situation where your client is telling you a negative or sad story about themselves. Their energy level is low, and they're telling you how bad their situation is. Your natural reaction, in an effort to be kind, is to join them on their energy level and say something like, "Oh, that's terrible, I'm so sorry to hear that."

Now you're both stuck in the dumps, and it's unlikely the conversation will take a positive turn. So how do you transform the energy from low to high? You can respond with a positive spin, such as, "Wow, I've never heard it that bad before, but I have to tell you, I've got to congratulate you for still having the willpower to want to make a change and want to make it different. That's impressive." Again, you've lifted the conversation by giving a compliment. You've made the person feel better about themselves.

Pace

What you'll learn is that every small element of what you say and how you say it has an effect on the conversation. The more of these elements you are aware of and master, the better salesperson you will be.

The pace of how you talk is one of these elements. There is an optimal words-per-minute rate at which you should communicate to have the best effect, the best influence on somebody. This notion is based on the science of how the human brain works and how it receives and processes words. The average and optimal speed at which you communicate should land between 140 and 160 words per minute.

If you're talking too slowly, the person you're talking to will easily get distracted, and they will lose interest. They will start typing emails, they will start checking text messages.

On the other hand, the average human brain does not have the capacity to absorb information at a rate above 160 words per minute.

There are outlier cases, of course. Tony Robbins typically speaks at around 200 words per minute. But in his case, he is very skilled at fluctuations and tonality to make sure his audience can absorb more words per minute. This way, he can present more content and increase his dynamic tone. But as I said, this is an unusual case that takes great skill to pull off successfully.

So, what does 140 to 160 words per minute sound like? Here is an exercise for you to try. Following is a paragraph of 160 words. Set a stopwatch for one minute, then read the paragraph out loud. Repeat the exercise until you can read the paragraph in as close to one minute as possible.

"Hi John, my name is Ron Jones. I got your number from our mutual friend, Andrew Jenkins, who sends his regards, by the way. The reason I am calling is that Andrew thought that you may be interested in a service that I'm offering. I work for a company called ABC Tech. We're based in Scottsdale, Arizona, and we offer a dog walking service. But what might be interesting to you specifically is that we specialize in walking smart! I looked at your LinkedIn profile, and I saw that you have a dog called Milo. I love that name, by the way, especially for a dog. You mentioned in your bio that your dog likes to walk three times a week. Interestingly, I might have a package that is perfect for you! We have a

special running at the moment for 3 walks a week at a 15 percent discount. Does this sound like an interesting idea?"

NEURO-LINGUISTIC PROGRAMING

The concept of neuro-linguistic programming is a powerful one, and I'd like to share it with you. You may have come across this term before (it's often abbreviated as NLP), as it's mentioned by many thought leaders and business coaches. Let's look at exactly what it is and how it can be applied to sales.

Let's start with the Wikipedia definition:

NLP's creators claim there is a connection between neurological processes (neuro-), language (linguistic), and behavioral patterns learned through experience (programming), and that these can be changed to achieve specific goals in life.

NLP is effectively the manipulation of brain coding; it's much like how computer programming works. Software programmers give a machine a code or instruction, and in return, they get a predictable response.

While the human brain is infinitely more complex than the most advanced computer, it is still quite similar to a "machine" that's been programmed—our brains are conditioned throughout our lives to give specific responses to specific prompts.

Let's consider a simple example. A child is constantly told by their mother that people who wear red socks are bad people. The child sees that every time their mother sees someone with red socks, she quickly walks away. This becomes code that's programmed into the child's brain. The child grows up and is now a corporate executive. He's interviewing a candidate for a job but notices the candidate is wearing red socks. The response is quite predictable.

Our brains are filled with all kinds of code—some quite odd things like the above example—but also many very common things. In some areas, most people have a similar basic operating system. An example of this is that most brains are programmed to perceive a loud and fast-talking voice to be aggressive, and therefore, our brains are coded to activate a defensive mode for protection.

A common theory among psychologists is that the majority of our brain's programming is set by the time we are eight years old. However, it's also widely accepted that our brains are "elastic" and can be reprogrammed.

The mastery of NLP can give you an exceptionally powerful skill. You can be as persuasive as the Jedi Mind Trick in *Star Wars*. In the movie, *The Matrix*, Neo gains the superpower of being able to see the "code" that makes up everything. The skillful salesperson has the ability to identify a person's brain coding and apply the right code to reprogram their built-in response.

Neuropsychologist Dr. Mel Robbins (no relation to Tony Robbins) explains in her famous book, *The 5 Second Rule*, that the average person struggles to make difficult decisions even when they want the desired outcome. She talks about a part of the brain that's called the "amygdala."

The amygdala is designed to shut down hard things. It's designed to protect you from doing difficult or dangerous things. It's the amygdala that is programmed to tell you, "Don't take that jump, it's dangerous," or, "Don't make that investment, it's risky," or, "Don't talk to that man in the red socks." According to Dr. Robbins, you have five seconds to override that response, and you override it through action.

The No

One of the great challenges that salespeople face is a piece of code that's imprinted into every human's brain. It's one of the first and most basic pieces of brain programming. And that is the word "no." This programming will typically develop when a toddler is between 18 to 36 months in age. At that point in their growth, their "ego" will begin to develop, and they become more aware of "me" and "mine."

At this stage of life, they will learn the power of saying "no," and often, they'll go through a period of saying "no" to pretty much everything (which is part of the joys of being a parent). We, as salespeople, need to learn how to put programming into people that will help them override their natural tendencies to say no. Sometimes a "no" is the literal word, but most adults will say "no" by using a sentence or two.

Commands

A computer programmer gives a computer commands. The commands in the programming language tell the computer what response to give, and the result is predictable. There are commands that you as a salesperson can use to also get the predictable results you want.

Here is an example: You're on the phone with a client, and you end the call by asking your client to discuss the idea with his spouse. You say that you'll call back the next day. When you call back, you may ask the question, "How did it go when you talked to your spouse?" Asking the question that way will result in a short, non-communicative response such as "It was alright."

A subtle language change in the way you can ask that question is: "Let's talk about how the chat went with your spouse. Tell me about it." Their brain is not receiving a question; you're sending it a command, and the brain will respond with a different result. The response you get will open up a space to have a conversation, rather than just a short answer that stifles communication.

Yes

I've said it before, but I'll keep repeating it because it's the most important word in sales. The word is "yes!" It's a word that needs to be embedded in your own brain's programming.

My philosophy for sales and also for life is a philosophy of "yes." If I'm asked something such as "Can you do this?" "Can that work?" my answer is almost always "yes." Here's why.

There is nothing on the other side of a "no." Literally, everything is on the other side of "yes." If you want to experience opportunity, if you want to get the most from everything you can in life, you need to learn how to say yes more often. That's a program you need to code into your brain. When you say yes more often, it's easier to expect and get other people to say yes more often.

What They've Done

One of my methods for using linguistic programming is a language pattern that I often use throughout my sales pitch. I constantly remind a client of what they've already done up to this point. I'll say, "John, by now, you have already enrolled in our community. By now, you have already had the chance to talk to one of our specialists. By now, you've probably already gone through and listened to some of our recordings."

There's a programming trick that's disguised in these sentences. I'm saying "by now," which sounds the same as "buy now." The client isn't aware of this, but their subconscious is picking up and getting used to this word. There's a famous master mentalist by the name of Darren Brown who is fascinating to watch. In his shows, he uses NLP techniques where he repeats disguised words. These words persuade the brain to give certain responses. It's not dissimilar to a kind of hypnosis.

Agreements

One of the most powerful and effective NLP strategies is to elicit "yes" and agreement responses from your client throughout the sales pitch. With each yes and with each agreement, you are programming the brain to activate its "yes" program. In my conversations with people, I will say, "John, today, I'm going to ask you a bunch of questions. I'm going to answer all your questions. I'm going to tell you all about our product. Then, we're going to find out if this is a good fit for you." And then I ask, "Is that fair enough?" The response will always be yes. I've elicited four important responses:

- First, I've gotten implied consent to ask them a bunch of questions and be a little bit invasive.

- Second, I have convinced them already I'm going to answer all their questions, no matter what they are, so they can take down their defenses.

- Third, we've agreed that I'm going to tell them all about my product.

- And fourth, we just made an agreement that we are going to see if this is a good fit.

I have programmed them from the beginning of my conversation. Toward the end of the conversation, we know what we're going to do. At the very end, I say, "John, do you think this is a good fit for you?" They've carried that agreement in their mind and know it's coming. They've connected the beginning to the end. That connection is satisfying. The brain has been programmed to expect that question, and when it's asked, the brain feels positive and satisfied. They will most often say yes.

Tone and Fluctuation

The tone and fluctuation of how we speak can mean a world of difference to getting the desired response. When I was in my early 20s, I studied Cantonese through Yale University. Cantonese is a beautiful language spoken in Hong Kong and the southern part of China. One of the interesting things about Cantonese is that it is a tonal language. There are seven different tones in the way you fluctuate your voice. This means that the same word can have seven totally different meanings. This can cause embarrassment if you're not careful. For example, the same word is used for "dog" and "penis," but only a change in tone differentiates which is which!

Does this happen in English? Does the way we say something and the tone of our voice change meaning? It sure does!

Let's look at an example. You arrive back home from the office and ask your spouse, "How was your day?" They reply, "Brilliant." But how they say "brilliant" can mean two different things. If they say "brilliant" with a bright and happy voice in a slightly higher pitch than normal, it genuinely means "brilliant." If they say it with a low tone and stretch the word out, then it's actually sarcastic and means "awful."

With sales, the tonality, the diction, the speed, and the cadence in which you communicate can program people. They will hear something different than what you say. If you're sitting down with somebody, and you want to really convey to them the intensity of the situation or the emotion of the situation, will you lower your tone? Will you slow the cadence of speech? Will you almost whisper? Absolutely.

No Buts

There are some words that should be removed entirely from your vocabulary, and one of these is the word "but." Inserting a "but" in a sentence will negate everything that has come before it. "But" has an aggressive, accusatory, distrustful connotation. It makes the conversation appear to be a competition to "win" an argument or appear more knowledgeable. The word to use instead is "and." It makes all the difference in the world. "And" means that you acknowledge the first point as true, as well as your argument.

Other No-No's

Most of us use a lot of superfluous when we speak. Typical ones are "like," "so," "um," and "sorry." Training yourself to remove these words greatly increases the sound of confidence in your voice. It's a useful exercise to record some of your conversations. Listen to the recordings and take note of the unnecessary words that you tend to overuse. It can be quite a surprise to discover how many of these "filler" words you are dropping into your conversation; most of us are completely unaware of them!

KEY TAKEAWAYS

- ➤ What you say matters just as much as **how you say it.**
- ➤ The skill of a salesperson is to **master the use of words.**
- ➤ Your customer is ALSO making a sales pitch. **It's your sales pitch vs. theirs.**
- ➤ **Influential Language Patterns** can help you take control of your conversation. For example: responding to the question "How was your day?" with a one-syllable word (e.g., good) will cut the conversation short, while a multi-syllable response (e.g., fantastic) will encourage further engagement.
- ➤ **Avoid negative-speak** by using positive and in-control language. For example, if you are late for a meeting, replace "I'm sorry" with "You've been patient."
- ➤ The **optimal pace** of your talking should be between 140 and 160 words per minute.
- ➤ The skilled salesperson is aware of **Neuro-Linguistic Programming (NLP)** and understands that all humans' brains have been "programmed" to

give specific responses. It is the job of the salesperson to "reprogram" their client's "brain code" by prompting with the correct words and phrases.

➢ Your **tone and fluctuation** have a great effect on your sales pitch.

➢ Remove the word **BUT** from your vocabulary.

➢ Build confidence by **removing superfluous words** such as "um," "sorry," and "like."

ACTION STEPS

➢ When the next person asks you how your day is, simply reply "good," and note how the conversation continues (or doesn't continue). Try this again with another person and reply "fantastic" and note any differences in the trajectory of the conversation.

➢ Record yourself talking about any subject that you know well. Speak for at least three minutes. Play the recording back and listen for which superfluous words you tend to use often (e.g., um, like, etc.). Try a second time and attempt to remove these unnecessary, filler words. When you are tempted to use them, simply pause instead.

CHAPTER 7

Challenge Them...Then Inspire Them

As a salesperson, every time you communicate with a potential customer, you have the opportunity to increase their buying confidence. You need to *inspire* them. To do that, you need to fill them with the urge to do something.

Your goal is to override the programming they have in their own head about why they cannot or should not buy your product. If potential customers had a natural or psychological need or compulsion to buy something, the world wouldn't need salespeople.

You need to challenge them to think differently than they normally would. Buying something for more than a few thousand dollars is hard for most people. It is not comfortable. They have natural resistance. Your job as a salesperson is to work with them to get them comfortable with the decision.

One way to do this is to show them how uncomfortable the alternative is.

THE PROBLEM

No matter what you say in your script, no matter how well you follow your outline, no matter what you say in your phone call or your presentation with a client, if you cannot identify what their problem is, you're going to struggle.

Whatever you are selling, ultimately, what you are really doing is solving someone's problem. Of course, don't assume that everyone you speak to has a problem that your product or service can solve. This can waste time for both the customer and you. Sometimes, when we're so engrossed in the benefits of our product, we start to think that everyone should say yes to it whether it's really right for them or not.

In the early stages of your sales conversation, before you start pitching, ask questions and listen carefully to find out what your potential customer's problem is. The litmus test is when you reach a point where you feel you could clearly explain their problem back to them. And often, it's quite a good idea to actually do this by saying, "John, I've been listening to you with interest, and from what I understand, your problem is that...am I correct?"

In some cases, the customer won't even be aware that they have a problem, and in that case, it's your job to show them the problem they aren't seeing. There's a brilliant example of this in the movie *The Wolf of Wall Street*. The star of the show is a brilliant salesman—in fact, one of the best in the world. He's giving a talk about sales and he begins it by asking the audience to sell him a pen. Members of the audience have a go at it, saying things about how lovely and useful the pen is—but it's clear that none of these attempts are working. Then we see how it's done. He hands a colleague a pen and says, "Sell me the pen." The colleague tells him, "Write down your name on this napkin," to which he replies, "Sorry, I don't have a pen." Boom! Sale done!

Digging Deep #1

A client's problem is not always as simple as not having a pen. It can often take quite a bit of questioning and digging deep to find out the true source of their problem. Again, many clients won't even be aware of exactly what their problem is.

I'm going to share an example with you. It's a little complex, but that's by design because sometimes problems are hidden among all sorts of other thoughts and information.

Let's say you're in the financial services industry, and one of your jobs is to sell mutual funds, portfolios, or retirement accounts. You're on the phone with John, and you begin by saying, "Hey John, what brings you to us today?"

John starts by saying, "Well, my portfolio really took a beating during the pandemic. It took a 60% hit during the decline, the recession in 2006, '07, and '08. It built back a little bit over the last 10 years, but 2020 really decimated my portfolio. I'm really looking for different vehicles that will help me in retirement."

So now you've got some information—John is worried about his retirement, and the crashes in the market have made him vulnerable. These are important pieces of information, but you still don't yet know the actual core problem that needs a solution. Be careful about making quick assumption. Sometimes the actual problem is not how it's first presented.

Let's look at some language and techniques that will help you dive deeper.

Your response should be along the lines of this: "John, thank you for sharing that with me. We have found that to be quite common with some of the clients we've talked to. Let me ask you, what problems did the downturn in 2006, '07, and '08 and the downturn in 2020 specifically create for you that you think we could solve?" Again, you're probing for the real problem. With each answer, you'll refine your next question, trying to drill down. If this takes the majority of your phone call, so be it; invest the time. This probing for the exact problem is the key to the kingdom. This is the secret sauce right here.

John's going to realize you're digging one layer deeper. It's going to make him a little bit uncomfortable. John's going to eventually tell you the truth. He's going to say, "Well, it's extended the age at which I can retire. I'm 67 right now, I thought I'd be retired by 65, but now based on the downturns in my portfolio, I won't be able to retire until I'm 73." There's a possible eight-year delay there that he's pretty frustrated about. Let's ask him more about that.

"What do you mean by that, John?" John's going to say, "Well, I was going to retire at 65 because I had enough in my retirement portfolio to carry me for 30 years, but when I took a hit on those things, I had to keep working and earning income, so I could support my family. Otherwise, I knew I would run out of money. If I had retired at 65, I would have had to start cutting steaks out of the budget."

Once you get all this information, you may think you know what the problem is, but you're not done just yet. Remember, you get only one real shot at saying what their real problem is and having them agree to what you say. OK, once you're ready, take a shot at verbalizing John's problem once you think you know the problem at this point. You might say, "John, do you mind if I repeat a little bit of what you said just so I'm really clear on what the problem is we're trying to solve?" and John's going to say, "Yes."

"What I heard you say is your portfolio took a downturn and that extended your working years by a possible eight years, and you need a financial product that is going to either stabilize the losses or can reverse those losses, so you can retire under a certain goal before you're 73. What age do you actually want to retire, John?"

He's 67. His original goal was 67, But he's already had to revise that. "What age do you want to retire?" "Well, realistically, I don't think I can do it in the next year or two. I'm going to shoot for 70. My goal is going to be when I'm 70."

You're going to say, "Okay, so what I heard you say is that through circumstances out of your control, your portfolio took a hit, and you have to extend your working years before retirement from 65 to 70. You're 67 now, and your goal is that your retirement account will have enough money in it so you can retire at age 70, which is three years from now. Is that the problem we're trying to solve?"

John's going to say, "Yes, that is what I'm trying to solve."

You've clearly identified what the problem is. Now, everything in your conversation from this point forward should be focused on a solution to get John to retirement by the time he's 70. Every example, every story, every product description, everything about your company, everything should be designed to solve John's specific problem.

This example is common in that often, the client hasn't grasped exactly what their problem is. It's often uncomfortable for people to dig deep, identify their problem, and say it out loud. This means that there are times where you have to ask challenging questions, even if this makes your customer a little uncomfortable. Sometimes your job is to inspire, sometimes your job is to challenge.

Digging Deep #2

Let's take another example, this time in the education industry.

You're selling micro-education products with which some-one can acquire an educational certificate within 8 to 12 weeks so they can get a higher-paying or at least a different job.

In this example, you're talking to a new, potential customer on the phone, and you begin with, "John, what can I help you with? What brought you here?" John replies, "Well, I was just looking…" If someone gives you this answer, and it's a really common one, you need to be really direct and honest with them and say, "I'm here to help you. What are you looking for?"

You've opened a conversation, and John replies, "Well, I'm trying to get out of my job."

The unskilled salesperson will think they have found ex-actly what the problem is, but the skilled salesperson will realize that there is further digging to do.

You're going to ask, "Why do you want to leave this job? What about it makes you want to quit?" John will say, "Well, I don't like this, and I don't like that," and you can respond along the lines of, "Oh, and what kind of problems does that create for you in your life?" This is known as "finding the pain." It causes some uncomfortableness because you're asking the customer to dig deeper and share more information—perhaps even think about things out loud that they haven't been brave enough to do.

John will explain his thinking further, and you will say, "John, thanks for sharing that with me. Do you mind if I repeat that just to make sure you and I are on the same page and I heard what you said?" and they always say, "Yes." This is actually very flattering to a customer. If you can repeat to them correctly what they said to you, what the problem is, and that you understand it well, then they're flattered you were listening so carefully.

The skilled salesperson has learned from experience how to actually articulate the client's problem better than they did. That's a powerful thing to do and will make the client thankful, engaged, and trusting. Your articulation of the problem should be molded to create an image in their head of just how acute the problem is.

But once you've explained their problem back to them, there is still further digging to do. The next question is, "How long has this been going on? How long have you been worried about it?"

John answers that he's been worried about it for the last five years. You respond by saying, "Whoa. Has that caused any other problems or challenges in your life—that stress hanging over your head for the last five years?"

John confirms that it indeed has. "Yeah, it's caused so many problems in my personal life. It's caused problems with my self-confidence."

The next thing to ask is, "How much money do you think you can make if you acquire this learning, acquire this skill set?" To which John replies, "Well, I've looked online. The average person in this field makes $20,000 more than I make right now."

Animatedly, you respond, "Wow, $20,000 more, and you've been thinking this for five years? That's not five years ago. That's $100,000 ago! I'm starting to see how this has become a problem, how this has become a challenge in your life." You've now shown John what it's actually cost him by not making a decision, and you've shown him how urgent it is for him to act.

You ask one more question before you move on: "John, what happens if you don't solve this? What happens in your life if you don't fix this problem?" This will be an uncomfortable question for John to answer, but it's important, and it will make him see the full picture—it will make him see how important it is to make a decision and fix his problem.

Let's think about value. Value doesn't come from describing a product in a certain way. Value comes from finding out someone's problem and fixing it. If the problem is big enough and painful enough and the solution is the right one, people will look beyond the cost.

Cost never matters if the problem is important or serious enough. We have a lot of kids in my family. Some of them break their wrists. Some of them get hurt. Some of them get sick. If I take one of my kids to the doctor and the doctor says, "Your child has a broken arm, and if you don't fix it, they will have a crooked arm for the rest of their life." Well, that's a succinct description of the problem. But I don't then think, "Hmm, let's see, if I don't solve the problem, he'll have a crooked arm the rest of his life but to solve the problem, I'll need to pay $10,000." I don't balance the cost against not taking action. The answer is, "Yes, fix it," no matter what, because the problem is serious enough or important enough for me to solve.

When you're talking to people about your product and your solution to their problems, you need to get into this "broken arm" zone. Their problem needs to be serious enough or important enough to them to solve despite the cost. Now, you have to trust that the provider of your product has a reasonable and value-marketed price, so you're not taking advantage of people. But in the end, if the problem is serious enough or important enough, price should never be an issue. Ever.

KEY TAKEAWAYS

As a salesperson, it is your job to:

➢ Inspire.

➢ Fill your client with the urge to do something.

➢ Challenge your client to think differently.

➢ Help them to be comfortable with their decision.

Dig deep to find the root of your customer's problem—it may not be what they say at first, and they may, in fact, not be aware of it themselves.

Only be satisfied with the answer once you can clearly say it out loud.

ACTION STEP

Talk to a friend, family member, or colleague about a dream of theirs that they have not taken action on (just about every human will have something). Talk them through the problem so you can understand why they haven't taken action and what the core problem for them is (using the guidelines and examples of this chapter). Once you have successfully identified the problem, repeat it back to them and see if they agree with your understanding.

CHAPTER 8

The Mechanics of Making the Sale

Fundamentals Win the Game

At one time, Tiger Woods was considered the best golfer in the world. As with any pro golfer, his mechanics for any particular kind of shot are exactly the same from one hole to the next. Imagine if, when Tiger approached every tee box, he changed his grip. On the first tee, he swings right-handed, and on the second tee, he tries it left-handed, then maybe with his hands in a different spot on the shaft. Can you imagine the silliness? He would surely not have won the tournaments he did if he changed his mechanics every time out.

Once we have a system that works, there's no need to change it. And continually repeating a proven system leads to mastering it further with more experience.

Sales is the same in this way. Learn the fundamental mechanics. Polish the process, and when you get it right, repeat it over and over! Don't pick up the phone and change your approach every time. If you do that, you will always be a beginner. Mastery of anything comes from the continuous repetition of a winning formula.

We'll delve into them in more detail, but first, here is a list of the basic mechanics for making a sale:

1. Be Professional.

2. Be Confident.

3. Learn Managed Language Patterns.

4. Show Empathy.

5. Follow a Script.

6. Ask the Right Questions.

7. Be Succinct.

8. Ask for the Sale.

9. Wrap It Up and Shut Up.

Fundamentals also include understanding the basic *emotional milestones* of a sales call. Each of these milestones must be checked off the list, or the client will not buy. Do them in order and check them off as you go.

1. Interest.

2. Excitement.

3. Agreement.

4. Committment.

5. Follow through.

THE FIVE EMOTIONAL MILESTONES

Many salespeople, when contacting a client, get "hypnotized" into repeating the same dialogue. It's easy to slip into the process of, "Oh, I've got a script. I need to say this and this and this." You check things off the list, get all the way through your regular script and then think, "I did what I was supposed to do. I said what I was supposed to say. Either it worked, or it didn't work." I think this is inaccurate thinking.

You can repeat the same script and it can have two totally different outcomes. But why? It's the same script! The variable ingredient is that there are emotional milestones you need to accomplish during your phone call. If you don't accomplish them in order, or if you skip over one of them, you're going to have a lower conversion.

Achieving these emotional milestones is not part of your script, per se. They are, however, so very, very vital. Let's look at them in further detail.

Interest

You need to establish as early on as possible in your phone call if the client is interested in what you're talking about. Don't mistake the fact that they are on the phone with you as being a sure sign that they are interested. This may not always be the case!

You need to ask them if they are interested. This can be done in a number of ways. For example, if you get 15 minutes into your conversation, you need to look at your emotional milestone checklist and ask yourself, "Wait, do I even know if they're interested?"

If they haven't given you some affirmation from their side that they are interested, you should stop and ask something along the lines of "You know what, I think we're getting ahead of ourselves. Let me ask you a question, John. Are you interested? Before I move forward, I just want to check that you are interested in learning more about..."

Sometimes, you're going to have to do what's called a *pattern interrupt*. We're going to have a whole section on pattern interrupts later, but here's what it sounds like: "John, the more we talk, I feel like I'm the only one talking, and I feel like you're not totally connected to this conversation." And with that pattern interrupted, they'll typically reply, "Oh, I apologize. I was doing emails. I'm back. I'm here." And that little pattern interrupt will get them connected and get them in line with what you're talking about.

Excitement

Salespeople often try excitement as step one, but the reason this step is the second step is that you can't get someone excited about a product if they're not interested in it, right? Once you've established interest, then you need to elevate their excitement about what you're selling. That can come in the form of an explanation, a testimonial, or making an offer. But whatever method you use, it's vital to elevate your potential customer's excitement level.

You can, in fact, ask them quite directly if something would get them excited. For example, ask them the question, "If we can solve this for you, would that get you excited?" If they say yes, then you can check the box. That's if you feel the excitement from them—if you can hear it in their voice. But never assume they're excited.

You might say, "John, is it just me or... by the sound of your voice, you sound pretty excited about this. Am I right?" And if he says yes, then you can check the box. You hit the interest milestone, and you hit the excitement milestone.

Remember that people are different and express excitement in different ways. Some people brighten up their voices and sound positive and upbeat. Others are more reserved and low-key about their excitement. If you suspect they are the latter, you could ask something like, "John, is that a little excitement I hear in your voice about what we're talking about?"

Agreement

"Agreement" is the third emotional milestone and this one is particularly important. It's a big one. This is the first opportunity you have to go for what we call a "mini" or a "partial" close. This is a temperature check.

At this point, you have established their interest, you know they're excited, you've identified their problem, and you've done some presentation.

Now it's time for prompting and agreement, and it sounds like this: "John, as we move through this conversation, if we are able to do X, are you willing to do Y?" Or you could get the client to agree that their situation can really no longer go on the way it is so you can ask, "Can we both agree you need to make a change, so we're not having this conversation a year from now?" Whatever your question, at this point, you're looking for them to say the word "yes." In some cases, you can push for even more than one agreement.

Commitment

Once you've made an agreement and gotten a "yes," you're going to go to one of the most important steps and ask for a commitment. This is where you're effectively going to close. This is ultimately what you are asking for, the sale, a "call to action." A call to action is not a "can you" question; it's a "will you" question.

Your question should be along the lines of "*Will* you move forward and take action on this?" or "*Will* you do exactly what you said and fill out the order form?" Once they've made the commitment, seal it in by repeating the commitment they've just made back to them. It's like a metaphorical handshake over the phone.

Follow Through

Going back to Tiger Woods, every golfer knows that the success of a shot is all about the follow-through. You can get every element right—you've chosen the right club, your stance is perfect, you've assessed the play—but if you don't follow through with your swing, none of the other things matter.

In sales it's the same. Every salesperson has had the experience of getting a client interested, excited, agreed, and committed, only to find that they never took action and made the payment.

Once you've gone through the first four steps and have closed the sale, it's tempting to give yourself a high five. But the truth is, a sale is only truly closed when a payment has been made. As they say, "Don't count your chickens before they hatch."

When you get that final "yes," this is just the beginning of your follow-through strategy. Once they say yes, you need to put in place a path to payment: "Okay, John. It sounds like you've got to go to the bank and get some funds straightened out, and we're going to talk tomorrow at 3:00. John, before I let you go, I know this is important to you, but I know life happens. If I don't hear from you tomorrow at 3:00, what am I allowed to say or what am I allowed to do that's going to reawaken you and get you to do this?" or "I want to help you follow through with your commitments. What can I say or what do I have permission to do tomorrow at 3:05 if you don't show up for a follow-up appointment?" I know that sounds really pushy, but they will appreciate it if you've done the rest of the phone call right.

Sometimes I even use myself as an example to show humility: "John, about a month ago I intended to sign up for something and I was so busy I totally forgot, and now I regret it. If I don't hear by 3:05, would you mind if I give you a call to remind you? I wish someone had reminded me!"

I'd like to share with you a personal story that I experienced with a follow-through that I'll always remember.

Many years ago, I was doing business in the South Pacific island of American Samoa. There was a nurse I was working with, and I was selling her an education program. She had a lovely name which I'll never forget, it was ~~Fara Utu~~.

Fara wanted to participate in one of our programs, and she said, "Ryan, Ryan. I'm going to do this. I'm going to do it!" And I said, "Great. Let's talk on Friday. We'll get your application all set up." She didn't show up for the appointment on Friday.

On Monday, I called her, and she said, "Oh, I'm sorry, Ryan. I will definitely show up on Wednesday." Well, Wednesday came around, and again she was a no-show. I had enough. I was upset, and I was a little bit impatient with Fara.

I called her up and said, "Fara, if you don't follow through with this, I'm going to make one more phone call to you. And in that phone call, I want to say something that will awaken something in you, that internally, you will want to do this more than me just asking you to do it. What do I have permission to say to you that's going to snap you into action?"

She replied, "Oh, don't worry, Ryan. I'll do it." I replied, "That's not good enough, Fara. What can I say to you if you don't follow through on this? I want to say something that will only connect with you. What do I have permission to say if you don't follow through?" She got really quiet, and she started crying, and she said, "Ryan, make it about my family." I felt instantly emotional, and I asked, "What do you mean by that? What do you mean 'make it about your family?'"

She said, "I was born and raised on this rock, and I always promised myself I would do better than my parents. I always promised myself I would get out. I would do something bigger and better. I would get off the island. I promised myself, and I promised my family, and I promised my mom I would do that." She said, "If you really want me to take action, remind me this is about my family." By the time she was done, we were both crying, and we had developed a real connection.

Sure enough, I actually had to call Fara a week later because she had disappeared again, and I said to her, "Fara, you know what this is about, right?" She said, "It's about my family."

She applied that day, she got admitted, and she joined the program the same day. It was this opportunity I had to make sure that she would follow through on. Just because she said yes, just because she was committed, just because she was excited, that did not mean I was going to complete the sale until I worked on a follow-through plan with her.

MECHANICS

Now that we've discussed the Five Emotional Milestones, the next thing to look at is the mechanics of your pitch.

These are the things we're talking about that make us better on the phone. Let's look at each step that's needed to make a phone call a success.

Expectations

The very first thing you want to do when you get on the phone is to establish expectations. Expectations will create relationships. Setting expectations is going to de-escalate people's natural defenses. If your client thinks you have something to hide or you're saving something for later, there's going to be a natural skepticism.

The way you establish expectations is to tell your client in advance what is going to happen on the phone call. Here's how this is done: "John, on today's call, we want to accomplish a few things, and here's how it's going to go. I'm going to ask you a few questions. I'm going to answer all of your questions. I'm going to tell you all about our product so you can make an educated decision, then we're going to see if this is a good fit for you. Fair enough?"

Once you've gotten their agreement, you have successfully set expectations. This makes the client feel comfortable since they know what to expect, and it sets you up neatly for your final closing script.

When you get to the part of your script that calls for you to close the sale, because you've previously set expectations and your client has agreed to them, you can say, "John, first of all I was able to ask you some questions, get to know you, really figure out what you're looking for, and in my opinion, this sounds like a great fit for you. I've been able to answer all of your questions to your satisfaction so that you can make an educated decision. I've described our product to you in detail so you know exactly why it makes sense for you. The last thing that we're going to do is we're going to find out if this is a good fit for you. John, based on the information we've discussed, based on your current financial situation, do you believe this is a good fit for you?"

The next part is sometimes one of the hardest things we have to do. And that is to shut our mouths. Be *silent*. Let the silence push your client into giving their answer.

If they say yes, you say, "Great. What do you think is the next logical step?" And you go into your close. If they say no, you'll need to figure out whether you asked the right questions or enough questions, whether you didn't answer enough questions, or whether they don't understand the product. Go back and investigate those three areas and find out where they're hung up.

This is not a script. Rather it's an outline of a phone call. It's a great way to take command and control of a call. It's a great way to have a structure to a call.

Questions

Once you've agreed on the outline and structure of the call, you're going to get it started by asking questions: "Let's get to it. John, to start the questions, I wanted to ask you..."

As you go through all those questions, you're going to write down the answers they give you. You're going to think very cerebrally and logically about what the answers are and whether they make sense. Is this, in fact, a good product for them? Is this a good fit for them? You're thinking about that in advance.

Then either introduce your product and describe it in detail or review it if they have watched it on a webinar, and then tell them:

"Hey, you know what. I've asked all my questions. Thank you so much for that. It really helps me get to know you a little bit better. Let's go ahead and answer all your questions, John. What questions do you have?"

My recommendation is don't answer the questions one at a time. Get all the questions and then go back and answer all of them at once.

Here's what that sounds like: "John, what questions do you have?" And John says, "Well, how much time is this going to take during the day for me to accomplish?" You reply, "Oh, great question. Time. That's a very common one. I like that. John, what's your next question?" John asks his second question: "Is it hard?" "Well, yeah, okay, good, effort. We'll put effort down. Good question, John."

You then continue: "OK, number three, John, what other questions do you have?" John asks, "Well, how much does it cost?" to which you reply, "Ah! I knew that was going to come up. What other questions, John?" "Do you have any funding options, or what are my options to make payments, or how do I pay for this if I don't have all the money up front?" You reply, "Oh, yeah. That one comes up a lot. I'm just going to write down funding. Let's make sure we tackle that. John, what else?"

Do you see what's being done here—you are letting John know that you are making a note of his questions and assuring him that you understand them. In turn, John understands that you are going to answer them once he has finished all of his questions. Getting John to ask all of his questions first and then giving all the answers succinctly afterward is a powerful tactic. Here are reasons why:

- John is not interrupted between each question, so he will have an easier time remembering all of your answers.

- Once he has asked his questions, it is more or less finite. He won't feel the need to keep asking endless questions (sometimes clients keep asking questions to avoid making a decision).

- When you get a chance to answer all of his questions in one go, it will give the impression that you have many answers, and with each answer, you'll be able to build momentum and raise the level of excitement.

Once John has finished asking his set of questions, you should say, "John, I appreciate all the questions because I have to tell you the more questions you ask and especially these detailed ones, it really tells me how serious you are. It tells me you've given this some thought, and quite frankly, it makes my job much easier." You can then continue,

"John, I've got a list of four or five questions here. They're all very good ones. John, do you think that if we went through each of these questions, and I was able to answer them and give you answers at a level of satisfaction where you felt comfortable with moving forward, does this sound like something you'd want to get started with?"

I have just paused. I have just held the answers at ransom, haven't I?

What that means is, I've got all these questions. They're reasonable questions, and I just made an agreement. I just made him an offer. I said, "John, if I answer all these questions to your level of satisfaction, will you move forward?" And John says, "Yeah, I will." You go, "Great. Let's go through and answer these, John. Time, effort, cost, funding, let's go through and answer these questions."

And at the end, you say, "John, it looks like we've gotten through your list. Would you say that I answered those to the level of satisfaction where you feel like you can make an educated decision to move forward?" John says, "Yes." And you go, "Great. Based on your financial situation, John. Is this affordable for you at this time?" "Yep." "Well, what do you think the next logical step is, John, to get started? Great. I'll pull out the order form."

You have a script of what questions you're going to ask. But you should also be sure to make a list of the questions *they* ask. Hold them in limbo. Go for an agreement, then answer the questions. It's a great tactic. It's a great strategy. It's something I've done for over 20 years.

You should not get on a phone call or be in any sales circumstance where you are not being *intentional* and *deliberate*. Remember those two key words.

You set the expectations. I'm going to ask you some questions, I'm going to answer your questions, I'm going to tell you all about our product, and we're going to see if there's a good fit for you. If you go through those things and go through your emotional milestones, you will radically change the confidence and structure of your phone calls.

KEY TAKEAWAYS

Basic Mechanics That Make a Sale:

1. Be Professional.

2. Be Confident.

3. Learn Managed Language Patterns.

4. Show Empathy.

5. Follow a Script.

6. Ask the Right Questions.

7. Be Succinct.

8. Ask for the Sale.

9. Wrap It Up and Shut Up.

Basic Emotional Milestones of a Sales Pitch:

1. Interest.

2. Excitement.

3. Agreement.

4. Commitment.

5. Follow through.

ACTION STEP

Practice talking with heightened excitement and enthusiasm to people around you. See if you can influence them to raise their excitement levels in response to yours.

CHAPTER 9

Measure Twice, Cut Once

The Formula for Self-Measurement

Sales oftentimes comes down to formulas, to mathematics. Many say sales is a numbers game. I don't necessarily believe it's a numbers game, but it is mathematical. The thing I like about math is that once you know the equation, all you have to do is plug in the right data to make it work. Sales comes down to two things, primarily: math and duplication. Once you figure out how to do it, then it's just a matter of how many times you can duplicate it, over and over again.

One of the most important aspects of your sales role is to accomplish certain things at certain times during the process. Below you'll find the three key performance indicators (KPIs) that can lead you to the success you are looking for and how to use them as tools to improve.

CONTACT PERCENT

A contact is defined as having two-way communication with a potential client. No matter what product you're selling, contact percent is the number of people you actually had two-way communication with as a percent of the number of people you were given to work with. In the old days, we called it "voice to voice," because all we did was pick up the phone, but now some of your contacts may be a two-way email or a two-way text or a Zoom meeting. Whatever tool you use, it has to be two-way communication with your client. That's how we define it.

You must measure your contact rate. This is a direct measurement of your strategy or your effort. If you are not contacting at least 60% or more of all your prospects with two-way communication, you are either: 1. Doing it wrong, or, 2. Being lazy.

Here's a simple example: If you're calling on people at 7:00 PM your time, and you're on the West Coast, but you're calling people on the East Coast, and it's 10 o'clock their time, that's a bad strategy. On the flip side, if you're on the East Coast and it's 8:00 AM your time, and you're calling people on the West Coast, and it's 5:00 in the morning their time, bad strategy.

You can sort your lead list or your client list by phone number or you can look at the area codes and see where people live. Just a simple idea, simple effort. Are you reminding people of your appointments? These are things that would fall under your contact strategy category.

Effort: Are you working hard enough? Are you even giving yourself a chance? Do you have enough at-bats? If you're not working hard enough, you can't complain about anything else. That's where everything starts... *effort*. It's very hard for your sales manager to train effort. This is something you typically have to bring to the table, but if your contact percentage is low, look at one of those two things or a combination of your effort and your strategy. This is a perfect way to diagnose how things are going for you.

YES PERCENT

How many of the people you talked to said yes? Your Yes Percentage is a direct measurement of your communication skills. At least 50% of the people you speak with should say yes, they want your product. If you are under 50%, then you need to work on your communication skills. How are you presenting? What words are you using? What questions are you asking? Do you have the ability to compel people to like or understand your product? This is a direct measurement of your communication skills.

COLLECTION PERCENT

How many of the people who said yes to you actually paid? Your Collection Percentage is a direct measurement of your follow-up and follow-through skills. You should be collecting on 30% to 50% of the people who said yes to you.

ANALYZING THE FORMULAS

The importance of these formulas is that you can use them to find out exactly where you need to improve. If you think about an entire sales conversation from beginning to end, there are many things that have to happen. If you're not getting the numbers you want if you're not getting the conversions, if you're not getting the results, do you need to deconstruct everything and start from scratch? Probably not. Your measurable gap between where you are and where you want to be probably falls within a very small skill set, so let's look at how to find out where you can improve.

If your contact percentage is high and your yes percentage is high, but your collection percentage is below 30%, then you've got very poor follow-up and follow-through skills or systems in place. This is typically true of the sales rep who communicates really well, and when somebody says yes, they do a victory dance all around their desk, and they forget to come back and collect the money.

If you're above 70% contact, you're above 50% yes, and you're above 30% collection, you're doing just fine. If you want to get better, start measuring where you can make the greatest inroads on these three categories and see which one you can focus on the most.

For some of you, you need more training on communication skills. For some of you, you need more training on your follow-up systems. Do you have staff support in place? Do you have a follow-up sequence? Do you have calendar invites? Do you have reminders, so you know when and how to collect on people? These are all really, really important things.

The first scenario that we're going to talk about is an example where you have 100 leads. If you have a client who is giving you 100 leads, here's what it's going to look like. You're actually going to have two-way communication with, say, 70 of the people, and 35 of them are going to say yes. Of those, let's say 30% of them actually pay, so you have 10 people (rounding down a little bit) who actually bought and paid.

Now 10 divided by 100 is a 10% gross conversion. I'm going to use gross because this was from the total number of people you were given. Ten conversions out of 70 contacted? This is 14% net. That means that you collected on 14% of all the people you talked to.

The people who you work for, the owner of your product, the owner of the marketing firm, will focus on one thing. They focus on cost per lead or "CPL." This is how much money it takes to create each one of those 100 leads. This is a formula they use to figure out if they are profitable or not. This is why it's so important to them.

If their cost per lead is $10, they're doing well. If their cost per lead is $10, they know that you, the sales rep, have to generate more than $10 per lead in revenue, so their measurement is Cost Per Lead, and your measurement is Revenue Per Lead. That's the focus.

Now, using our numbers from above, how does it play out in the grand scheme of things? If you're selling a $4,000 product, that means your revenue per lead is 10 sales multiplied by $4,000. Your 10 sales at $4,000 are going to generate a total of $40,000 in revenue. Now, if we take that $40,000 of revenue and we divide it by the 100 leads the client gave you, you can see you have generated, on average, $400 per lead.

Now some companies expect more from you. I've worked for corporations, and you'll see this more in corporate sales, where you're on a salary. They're generating leads at $3 each. Sometimes they're looking for a 20 times ROAS (Return on Ad Spend) or a 10 times ROAS. In most of your online digital marketing categories, a really good baseline to start with, just to know that you're doing okay, is a three to four times return on ad spend.

That's why we look at these types of numbers. If you don't know what is expected from you, if you don't know that your sales manager expects a three or four times return on ad spend, you're looking for answers to questions you haven't asked, and that's a silly way to do it.

Sit down with your sales manager and say, "What is this number supposed to be? What is this revenue per lead supposed to be?" If they tell you it needs to be $400 and you're selling a $4,000 product, then sit down and reverse engineer everything and figure out what your numbers need to be. You can aim for those with laser focus.

KEY TAKEAWAYS

➢ Sales success is about refining your formula until it is perfected and can be replicated.

➢ Your sales success can be measured by the following KPIs:

➢ Contact Percent.

➢ Yes Percent.

➢ Collection Percent.

ACTION STEP

If you are already in a sales career, analyze your performance based on the above KPIs and take the necessary steps to alter your performance based on the results.

CHAPTER 10

Scripts = Success

Even Your Customers Have Scripts They Use

A script is a guide or road map. It is the best way to create a predictable outcome. I have heard many times that people don't like scripts because they don't want to sound "robotic" or like they are reading something.

Here's a Truth Bomb in 3, 2, 1…If you sound robotic, it has nothing to do with the script. It has everything to do with you and your communication style. If you are not following a prescribed and proven process (script) every time you talk to a potential customer, you will sound like an amateur every time! Think about actors—they follow a script. A Shakespearean theatre actor follows a script down to every single word—but they don't sound robotic, do they?

Here is a simple guide on how to use a script for any product or service.

A script gives you a baseline. It gives you consistency. It gives you that thing you're going to go to every single time. When I was on the phone doing phone sales, I can remember the months I did really, really well, I was following my script. I said the same thing every single time. When somebody picked up that phone, my introduction, my opening were the same every single time.

Once it works, don't change it. One of the best ways to make it work is to follow a script.

I remember the months where I had great sales. One month, I was number one on a team of 500 people. I'll never forget it. But I got a little cocky. I got a little lazy, and the next month, I thought I was so good at what I did that I just sat back and talked to people.

I went from number one to number 250 in less than 30 days! I was horrified! The reason why was because I got so comfortable and I got so cocky with my success that I stopped using my script. All of a sudden, I had convinced myself that people wanted to hear me talk. But the truth is, they wanted to hear my script. Because my script worked. And every time I used it over and over and over again, I got predictable results.

I asked you earlier what's the next objection you're going to hear on your next phone call? How do you know what they're going to say? You don't really know. But experience shows that most calls are the same because you've heard it before over and over.

You know what they're going to say with almost certain predictability because the people you are talking to are using a script, too! Their story about why they haven't started something, their story about why they can't have something, their story about not being able to pay for it, their story about thinking about it, their story about talking to a spouse, they have practiced these scripts over and over and over again. They've practiced these scripts on their friends. They've practiced them on their spouses and even the family pet.

Well, you know what your customer is going to do in real life? They're also going to try out new scripts. After talking to a salesperson, they may say to themselves, "Hmm, they didn't believe it when I said that. I need to change the way I said it because I need them to believe this story about why I don't have something or why I don't deserve something." And, the next time they deliver it, they'll change the way they do it.

This doesn't make your customer a bad person. This doesn't make them disingenuous. I promise you if somebody says they don't have the money, or "I have to think about it," if they have to talk a spouse, I promise you as sure as I sit here, this is not the first time they've said it.

"Wait a minute, what? They've been practicing this rejection? They've been practicing these objections over and over and over with everybody they have ever met?" And the answer is yes.

Think about your experience with these scripts in your head in your own life. Most of us have, at some point in our lives, had a script about why we can't do something. Let's take a typical example. Perhaps when you were younger, you were pretty good at playing the electric guitar. Now that you're older, you reminisce with those around you that you'd love to pick up the guitar again as a hobby because you really enjoyed it.

Your spouse says, "Do it! It will be a fun way to relax, and you've always talked about it." Truth is that you're a bit nervous that you won't remember how to play and people won't be as impressed as when you tell them about it.

So you say, "A guitar is expensive, and then I have to buy an amp too. You know what, I'll wait till I get that promotion and get more money." Your spouse does some research and says, "Hey, I found a guitar that's only $250. We can easily afford that!" Now you need to change your story.

When your friend Dave suggests you get started with the guitar again, you tell him a different script. "I'd love to, and it's not that expensive, but my real problem is time. I'm just so busy at work, and then I need to spend time with the kids..." I bet you relate to this kind of story. Most of us do.

Let's continue with this example of John and his guitar dreams (OK, maybe a little silly, but since we've got the example going and it's relatable to most of us...)

You're selling electric guitars, and you're on a phone call with John. As a salesperson in this niche, you should be aware of the common "scripts" that clients have. They're often very similar.

In this case, John gives you his first practiced script "I don't really have the money at the moment." Now the thing is, John knows that he actually does have the money. As a salesperson, you're not allowed to ever lie. That can get you in a whole lot of hot water. But as a client? You're free to tell lies; it's unregulated. And people often do as part of their practiced script.

John then proceeds to tell you his second part of his script: "The other thing is that I just don't have the time to practice, between my work and my family commitments."

INTERRUPT THEIR PATTERN

The tool that you have as a salesperson is to interrupt the pattern. If you allow your client to talk freely and run through their practiced script, you're allowing them to talk themselves out of the decision. After all, they've done it many times before, and they're really just repeating their story. And their story always ends in a negative. They already know that once they've explained themselves, they'll make a deep sigh and say, "I guess I'll look at it again next year."

What does a pattern interrupt look like? You can interject with a question and force the script to change. For example, you can say, "John, what would playing the guitar again really mean to you? What do you think the positive effects would be on your life?" Now, this question forces John to stop his practiced script and think about what he's saying. It's challenging him. It sets him up for a new conversation he hasn't had before. You've done a "pattern interrupt."

John will feel like his brain has short-circuited! He's being forced outside of his comfort zone and it now requires him to go off script and into unchartered territories. He will want to steer the conversation with his practiced script, but the more you interrupt his pattern, the further he will stray from his story, and the more opportunities will arise for you to change his internal narrative.

Not having money and not having time are common objections that clients will have, so you should have a script planned in advance for how to deal with these statements. For example, you might say, "John, I know where you're coming from. So many clients I speak to have the same problem. But something that's been interesting with my job is that when I talk this through with people that seem to have similar life pressures as you, they actually realize that there is a perfect time in the week for playing. Is there a time in your week for 'me' time? For example, what do you usually do on a Sunday evening?"

Another "escape" script that many clients use is, "Let me think about it." This is a dangerous one to allow as a salesperson because, as most salespeople know, ending a conversation with "let me think about it" usually means a lost sale. "Let me think about it" is the same thing as saying, "I'm not interested anymore. I just don't want to be convinced. I'm returning to my own practiced script, and it always ends with an 'I can't.'"

In this case, you could reply by saying, "John, in my experience, when you go think about it, all you're going to come up with is questions, but you won't have the answers, so why don't we do a little exercise right now. Tell me what kind of questions you think will come up after our call, so I can resolve them now, so you don't have to go think about it." You've interrupted their pattern.

If they say, "I need to talk to a spouse," there are many ways you can handle a spouse objection. If this happens to you regularly, in the beginning of your call, you can simply say, "Hey, John, you sound very excited about this. Is there anyone else you need to consult with before we move forward to make a decision?"

"Well, yeah, I need to talk to my spouse." "Great, why don't we put them on the phone and that way I can answer their questions, too. What kind of questions do you think your spouse would have that we can resolve, so you're better equipped to have that conversation?"

Interrupt that pattern. Don't just accept the story.

If they say money is an issue, interrupt that pattern. One thing you could say to them is, "Well, if you have no money, the first thing I want to tell you is congratulations because if you truly have no money and you're still making this phone call, that tells me you have not given up. It tells me you still want more. It tells me that you're not satisfied with saying, 'I can't afford it.'"

"John, how soon do you want to stop saying, 'I don't have any money?' And how soon are you willing to get started on something, find the money, and make it happen? Because those are two different directions we can go today, John."

To pattern interrupt, use words like "logical" or "thinking about it." If somebody says, "I need to think about it," I will take them down a path of analytics. I would say, "John, I'm glad you're going to think about it. That tells me you're very serious. Let's answer some of those questions right now because, by the time we're done, we're going to find out what you think the next logical step is. John, what kind of things would you be thinking about?"

Go through the whole list, resolve them. At the very end, come back and say, "Well, now that we've gotten through that, John, what do you think the next logical step is?" Subconsciously and consciously, I promise you the next logical step in their script is "let me sit on this," procrastinate and go think about it and just never talk to you again. That's not logical. The next logical step is, *Let's get started.*

If you can walk into a sales conversation knowing they have a script and be prepared to interrupt that script, to break that pattern, you're going to have a very good phone call and you're probably going to build a lot of trust with your customer.

KEY TAKEAWAYS

➢ It's vital to have a script and use it as a baseline for all sales pitches.

➢ "Pattern interrupt" your client to deviate them from their "script" and arrive at a different outcome.

ACTION STEPS

Talk to a friend, family member, or colleague about a dream they have that they haven't followed through on. For example, they may have always wanted to write a book, or pick up the guitar, or learn to paint. Listen to their "script" as to why they can't do that thing and use pattern interrupting language to challenge their practiced thought pattern.

CHAPTER 11

The Perfect Intro

I believe that first impressions matter. And I believe the way you open your call, the way you introduce yourself, and the way you introduce the call, will have an effect throughout the conversation. In fact, I think if you have the correct introduction, it can have amazing influence on your closing. So, if you open the call correctly, it is going to help you close the call correctly. Let's look at how to write, craft, or script, the proper introduction.

I believe your introduction can solve a lot of issues and objections that might otherwise come up.

Imagine you walk onto a car lot and a salesman walks up to you. And they do all the wrong things. They do their best Joey impression and great you with a cheesy, "How you doin'?"

Then, before even introducing themselves, they look at you and say, "What would it take to put you in that car?" Or worse, they have one car in mind because it gives them the most profit, and they're going to try to push you into that direction. Or you come on the lot and you say, "I'm looking for a blue, four-wheel-drive truck," and they start by showing you a white two-whee-drive Prius.

My theory is people don't like the car lot experience because there is this underlying belief that you don't know how much money the car salesman is going to make or how much money the dealership is going to make on that car. You feel like you will get taken advantage of. It's a big-ticket purchase. You're spending $50,000 on a truck. You don't know if they bought it for 40 grand and they're making 10 grand, or if they bought it for 49 thousand and are making just a thousand bucks. You feel like car salesmen are simply there to extract money out of your wallet.

That creates this inherent level of distrust. I'm going to describe to you a more skillful car sales experience. Imagine John comes onto a car lot, and I am a car salesperson. I walk up to John and I say, "How are you today?" John says, "I'm doing great." And I say, "John, I'm here to help you out. And before we get started, let me just kind of explain how things work at our car dealership. First of all, tell me, have you already decided to buy a car, and you're just looking for the right one, or are you still trying to decide whether or not you need a car right now in your life?"

John says, "Nope, I've decided I'm going to buy a car. I just need the right one." Then I might say, "Hey, perfect. Thank you for sharing that with me. This is going to make our experience much better. John, here's a piece of paper. And on this paper, you're going to see a list of all of our cars. And you're going to see a bunch of columns with numbers. And each one of those columns shows certain dollar amounts."

I then continue to explain, "Next to this car right here (let's say it's a Chevy Malibu), the very first column you see is the retail price of the car; the retail price is what's on the sticker, it's called the manufacturer's suggested retail price, the MSRP. That is the highest dollar amount you're going to see. Now, in the column next to it is another set of numbers. This set of numbers is what's called the invoice price.

"Now, many people think invoice price is the actual price that we as a manufacturer paid for it. That's not entirely true. But it's a little bit lower than retail price. Now in the column next to the invoice price is what we call our pack price. Pack stands for the amount of money that the dealership has packed into the price of the car so that we can afford to pay for the lights, we can pay for the receptionist, we can pay for the computers, and things like that. This is where the dealership has to guarantee their money; it's a little bit lower than invoice price."

I nod and smile genuinely, and John nods and smiles back to let me know he's with me. And then I continue explaining:

"The final column, this fourth column over here, this is the rock bottom price. This is the 'We don't make any money' price. And when I say we don't make any money, it only means that we don't make money over what we bought it for. But John, I want you to remember that we're a dealership that works directly with a manufacturer. And if we sell 100 units of this car this month, we get a rebate of 15% on everything we sell.

"So even if we lose money, we're still going to make 15% on the rebate back from the manufacturer. John, I'm going to give you this paper. And you're welcome to look at the lowest number on the columns. But you're also welcome to look at the highest number. I can tell you that if you find the car you want, you and I are going to have a conversation, and we're going to figure out somewhere between the column on the left and the column on the right that you're going to pay for that car.

"And if I can make a reasonable offer to you and you like it and you like the car, you like the price, I think we can do business today. Is that fair enough, John?"

John thinks, "Did I just walk into the twilight zone of awesome car sales experience? That was amazing!" John now knows exactly how the process is going to go. I'm going to end my introduction by saying, "Hey, John, I'm going to go and sit down over here and just wait for you to sniff some cars. When you see something you like, I'll take you for a drive. Or if you want, I can walk you around, introduce you to some cars and show you some. How would you prefer this experience to go?" And John says he wants me to walk him around.

THE IMPORTANCE OF INTENTIONS

There are two things you want to accomplish in any introduction.

Number one is you need to identify your intentions and you need to get them to identify their intentions. This is very important. Your introduction needs to accomplish those two things. If you can do those two things, you will immediately know if the two of you are on the same page.

Okay, so remember the first question that I asked John. I said, "John, have you already decided to buy a car and you're just looking for the right one, or are you still trying to decide whether or not to buy a car?" That question is designed to get the customer to identify their intentions. And it tells me where to go in my journey. Now, after that, I am going to tell John what my intentions are.

Before I do that, first let me tell you my secret to success in sales. You ready for this? *Tell the truth.* I could write a book on how to be a successful salesperson using just one sentence repeated over and over: Tell the truth. If you can tell the truth, you're going to do really, really well in sales.

But hear me out. When I say tell the truth, I don't just mean don't lie. I mean, tell the whole truth. Here's an example of not telling the truth that may surprise you. "Hey, John, this is Ryan. I'm calling today to answer all your questions." That's not a lie. But it's not the whole truth. The whole truth is that I am here to ASK you some questions. I'm here to tell you all about our product. And I'm here to see if that's a good fit for you.

In my introduction, I am going to identify fully and transparently what my intentions are, and then I'm going to translate it for you. "John, let me tell you how this is going to go today. And then we'll move forward." John says, "Great." You go, "John, first of all, I'm going to ask you a bunch of questions. Second of all, I'm going to answer all of your questions. I'm going to tell you all about our product or service. And we are going to see if this is a good fit for you. Fair enough?"

Now, let me translate what John and I just agreed to, and let me translate what my intentions are. This is what I just said to John, in different words.

"Hey, John, there's a bunch of information I need from you. And I'm going to ask you some questions to find out if you're a good fit for our program. I'm going to answer all your questions to a level of certainty, so you're comfortable with buying from us; I'm going to tell you all about our product and the problems that it can solve for you.

"Most importantly, we are going to see if this is a good fit for you. And later on, I'm going to ask you if this is a good fit for you because I'm going to ask you to buy our product."

That's what you're telling them. That's full transparency. Your introduction can set the stage for a close later on. When you introduce the call, no matter how you start your call, your introduction must end by your concluding, "When this is all over, we are going to find out if this is a good fit for you."

Imagine later on when it's time to do your close if all you had to say was, "John, I think we've checked all the boxes. Do you feel like this is a good fit for you?" John's going to say, "Yes, absolutely." And then you're going to go, "Great. Go grab your wallet, I will open up the order form and I'll walk you right through it."

Your introduction sets up your close. Your introduction must create a level of confidence in your customer. It must set up a level of certainty with them. You see, we are only afraid of what we don't know. But yet there's this optimism inside them that they want this to be too good to be true.

However, there's a certain level of distrust in the beginning of the call. When you identify your intentions openly and honestly with them in the beginning, then it removes that distrust; it actually removes that fear. You see, we are only afraid of what we don't know.

The other thing we're afraid of is the future. You can't be afraid of the past because it's already happened. And you can't be afraid of the present because you're in it. People are afraid of what's going to happen next. And you won't have a true connection, or you won't be building buying confidence in your customer unless you identify your intentions and remove that level of uncertainty.

Once you remove the level of uncertainty, you've built a relationship, you built rapport, and they will trust you as you're talking.

How do you build that trust? First of all, you're going to get them to identify their intentions. Basically, the question is, why are you here? You're going to get them to identify their intentions, then you're going to identify yours.

I'm going to ask you a bunch of questions, I'm going to answer all your questions, I'm going to tell you all about my product. And we are going to see if this is a good fit for you. Now, we have both identified our intentions. What if during your fact-finding, when you're trying to get them to identify their intentions, they're really not interested? Does that change the course of your call? Of course, it does. That's good information. You've found out in the first three minutes of your call.

Here's the real tricky thing. This is where one of your arms is tied behind your back. You are required to tell the truth.

They are not. When you are trying to get somebody to identify their intentions, there's a high probability they're going to lie to you, or they're going to give you a half-truth answer at first.

When you're trying to get them to identify their intentions, make sure you're asking questions that will probe and dig. Not uncomfortably, not unprofessionally. Just make sure you get enough information to where you actually know why they are on the call.

The only acceptable answer of why they're on a call is because they think, with a high level of certainty, that there's a possibility your product can solve a problem for them. And rarely are you going to say, "Why did you make this appointment? Why are we on this call?" And they're not going to say, "You know what, I've got a problem, and I hope you're going to solve it," they won't say that. They're going to say, "Oh, I just wanted to get some information." And you're going to go, "Awesome. I think I can handle that. Why do you need this information? What will it do for you in your life?"

"I think it'll help me. It'll help me in my job." "Tell me a little bit more about that. How could this help you in your job?" They aren't going to give you a deep, honest answer right at the start. They'll get to an honest answer layer by layer as you dig deep enough to stitch them all together so you can get a clear picture of what their true intentions are. Once you have done that, once they have identified their true intentions, and you know exactly why they're on the call, then you get to give them good news.

You say, "Well, John, I have great news for you. Based on what you're here for and how this call is going to go, I think we're going to be able to help each other, and I think you're going to enjoy it. Let's go ahead and get started." And then start asking your questions.

PROXY SELLING

One thing you don't want to happen is what I call proxy selling. This is when you may have the opportunity to sell to the higher-ups, the board of directors, or a management group, but a gatekeeper, a middle person, doesn't want to give you direct access and insists on delivering your sales message for you. That's not going to work. What you need to do in that case is sell the gatekeeper on who you are. Not the product, but sell them on who *you* are. You need to convince this middle person that nobody's going to present your product as well as you can. You need to let them know, to say to them, "I'll give you the information, but I'll tell you right now, you can't sell this product as well as I can."

If they wanted to sell by proxy, you would have to, inside of 30 or 45 minutes, give them enough information to become a professional salesperson, so good at what they do and so knowledgeable about your product that they could turn around and sell it to a board of directors. That doesn't make sense to me. And I'd have a strong conversation with yourself about whether you're in the right industry because, personally, nobody will sell it better than me.

And I don't want a gatekeeper of any kind trying to sell my product to a board of directors. What I want that person to do is go to the board and say, "Hey, I had a great conversation with Ryan. He works for ABC Company, they sell this product. I've gotten this information about what they offer. This guy is really professional, he's really good at what he does, I believe he can help us, and I think we should give him the time of day to talk to you guys." That's what I want.

INTRODUCTION SCRIPT

A perfect introduction needs to be scripted. It needs to be succinct, and it needs to accomplish those two things—identify your intentions, get them to identify theirs. If you can write a very succinct introduction, you will set yourself up to be in a great position. Once you have it, repeat it over and over and over and over again; don't ever change it.

When you get on the phone, you should say the exact same thing over and over and over. You should never change it. Now, that comes with one caveat. You should play with it until it gets good because practicing a flawed script doesn't make perfect; practice makes permanent. So, if you're doing it wrong, you've got to tweak it and evolve it and split-test what you are saying. Get your introduction dialed in so that it works and it works every time.

When it works every time, that will build your confidence. You can use it every single time because when your confidence goes up, the buying confidence of the client goes up.

A script creates predictable, duplicatable results. And in sales, that's what you want. You want to create duplicatable results. "Hey, John, this is Ryan. We had an appointment today at three o'clock you had scheduled and requested we call you to give you more information about our product and service." Notice I put it on them. *They* booked the appointment. They're the ones who inquired. I'm not cold calling. I didn't randomly find them. We didn't just both pick up the phone at the same time. We didn't both jump on Zoom at the same time. Language—*you* requested to talk to us.

"I am really excited to be on the call today. Let me tell you how this is going to go." Obviously, you'll exchange pleasantries first. "I'm going to ask you a few questions. I'm going to answer all of your questions. I'm going to tell you all about our product. And in the end, we're going to see if this is a good fit for you. Fair enough?" And John says, "Yes. Fair enough."

And you go, "Great. Let me get started by asking some questions. John, have you already decided that you're going to go back to school at this time in your life and you're just looking for the right education program? Or are you still trying to decide whether or not you are going to go back to school at this time in your life?" And then we're going to move on.

The introduction will probably go back and forth between the two of you until they identify their intentions. You can identify your intention in less than three minutes. But you have launched an opening to a conversation that was strong. It was succinct. It was confident, and they will respond and love it.

The introduction will play a major role in the overall outcome of the call. Your introduction must be clear, strong, inviting, and polished. Nothing will destroy buying confidence faster than a salesperson bumbling through an unprepared introduction.

After you complete all your required compliance pieces, like who you are, where you are calling from, and a notification that the call is being recorded, what you say next sets the tone for the rest of the call. If someone has inquired, applied, bought, or scheduled time with you, then make it clear they are the ones who requested this meeting.

> Wrong way: "I am calling to see if you would like to…"

> Right way: "John, you asked us to give you a call to discuss…"

INTRODUCTION TONE

While what you say in your introduction script is vital, starting with the right tone is also equally important. I find that an effective introduction is one that builds momentum. Sometimes when you are making call after call, your introduction can start to sound quite flat. It's highly effective if you start your call with positive and excitable energy. Your tone should tell them that you're fresh and alive; it should not sound like you are making your 20th call of the day.

Sometimes, to get this animation in my voice, I get up off my chair, walk a few paces away, and then walk back to my phone with a spring in my step and pick it up. Putting momentum in your body puts momentum in your voice.

KEY TAKEAWAYS

> ➢ Your introduction is one of the most important aspects of your sales process.

> ➢ Perfect your introduction script and use it again and again.

> ➢ In your introduction, you should:

> • Display positive and excitable energy.

> • Identify *your* intentions and get the client to identify *their* intentions.

> • Be honest and transparent upfront.

> • Set up your close by explaining how the conversation will go.

> • Build client trust.

➤ If you are selling by proxy, you need to convince the middle person that no one can explain the product/service better than you.

ACTION STEP

Work on your introduction script. Record your voice and note whether your words and tone of voice display positive energy.

CHAPTER 12

Finding Their—And Your—Motivation

Asking the right questions is a sure-fire way to make your calls more impactful and more effective. Questions are the guiding tools of successful sales reps. At our company, we teach the Socratic method of sales. This is a question-based technique.

A prescription without a diagnosis is called malpractice. If you try and sell a product or service to someone before understanding what problem you are trying to solve, you will have to cram it down their throats. This is <u>not</u> best practice. Asking the right questions in the right way will give you a much easier sale, and the client experience will be top shelf!

So how can you frame the right questions in the right way? You need to determine the customer's motivations.

Motivation is about reasons, that is, the reasons why you do anything. I like to put it in words that stick in my head. When I think of motivation, I think of "the motive to take action." To me, that helps me better understand in my brain and in my heart what motivation is. It's finding the motive to take action.

I want you to suspend your understanding and your belief of that just for a second, and I want to go into some different types of motivation. There are basically four primary types of motivation in humans. There is extrinsic, which means external; there's intrinsic, which means internal; there's introjected motivation; and there's identified motivation. Those are the four.

Extrinsic or external motivation is motivation that comes from somebody telling you to do something, or an external threat. For example, I always tried to motivate my children through various cajoling (and threats!) to get better grades—an external motivation to them.

The second type of motivation is internal motivation. This is when you know something is right, or you feel absolutely compelled to do it, or you do it for personal satisfaction. This is what we call inspiration. You are inspired to do something. This is intrinsic motivation. I did it because I knew it was the right thing to do, and I needed to better my life.

Introjected motivation is similar to internal motivation, but originates from a different source. Intrinsic motivation comes from you being inspired. Introjected motivation comes from feeling guilty for not doing something. I am motivated to take out the trash because I will feel guilty my wife has to do it instead if I don't. Introjected motivation is when you do it because not doing it creates a sense of guilt.

The last is identified motivation, which springs from you identifying something that needs to get done, for whatever reason, but has not yet been done. You've identified a task. You've identified a goal. You have a motive to take action, which is to get it off your list and to get it done.

These are the four types of primary psychological motivations. The ones we're told to do, the ones we're inspired to do, the ones we feel guilty for not doing, and the ones where we just know what needs to get done.

What I would encourage each of you to do is, in your own personal life, figure out what your goals and aspirations are and try to categorize where your motivation comes from. What motivates you to get up in the morning? What motivates you to go to the gym? What motivates you to make one more phone call? What motivates you to ask one more question when you're on a sales call? What motivates you to be a better person? What motives you to have to take action?

Motivation is largely a mental thing. Obviously, it's an energetic, mental type of thing, but one thing I want you to remember is that motivation, without action, is just good intentions. Motivation that is not coupled with action is useless. A motive is something that compels you. This motivation should compel you to *do* something.

CUSTOMERS AND THEIR MOTIVATIONS

When a client is talking to you, they're going to tell you what their motive is to take action regarding the product you're selling. You can quickly categorize this motivation. Is it an external thing? Were they told to do it? Does it come from within?

Here's what external motivation would sound like: "Hey, John, what compelled you to call me today?" "Well, my buddy did it, and he said, I should give you a call." His buddy gave him a motive. His buddy told him. That's an external motivation. Personally, I think that's kind of weak sauce. It's not as strong as the next one.

The next one is internal motivation. If you say, "John, what compelled you to get on this call today?" They answer, "You know what? I just felt inspired to do it. I felt like this year is going to be the year I need to do something big and I need to do something great. I've always wanted to do this. I just had this internal drive to make it happen." Now we're talking about some deep-rooted motives to take action! Those are the kind of people you love working with.

The introjected kind of motivation is revealed along these lines: "Hey, John, why are we on this call today? What compelled you to be here?" John says, "Man, I always promised myself I would do this, and I would just feel awful if I don't get it done. I'll feel awful if 2022 comes around and I haven't taken any steps towards my goal." Can you see the guilt showing up in that response? Again, not the strongest type of motive to take action, but it is compelling.

Fear can be a motivator. Not all motivation is deep-rooted and highly productive. If you say, "John, what compelled you to be on this call today?" John says, "Well, it's November 24th, and I had a goal to accomplish something this year, and I just haven't done it, and I want to make sure I get it done before the end of the year."

As a salesperson, you'll start to see the language patterns that will help you identify which of these four motivation types are driving your customers. It's my belief that if you can practice this and if you can really hone in on people's motivations, it's going to give you the ability to dig deeper in your phone calls.

If you're on the phone with somebody and you ask them what is compelling them to talk to you, and their answer is based on external motivation, I'm going to tell you right now those are the people who are most likely to flake on your next appointment and they won't buy.

They have the least potential for buying from you because being told to do something, being required to do something, will never ever be more powerful than being *inspired* to do something. I think we've all been in that category, right? Have you ever been required to do something, and you had a little bit of resentment towards it as opposed to being inspired to do something for which you felt great love and connection? Two totally different things.

I share that with you because if somebody expresses an external motivation for talking to you, then you will really need to question them deeper. Let's say I'm talking to

John, and I say, "John, what compelled you to make this call? What compelled you to make this appointment?" John says, "Oh, my buddy told me about it. He said it'd be a great thing for me to do." That's not a good enough reason, folks!

In such a case, I'd continue with some deeper questioning. I would start peeling back the layers of the onion. I would say, "Well, why do you think your friend thought this would be a good call for you to make?" "Well, he thinks that he knows I've always wanted to do this, and he knows that I haven't done it yet." Boom, now we're talking about identified motivation. Although we're not there yet.

We want to get to the inspired motivation. You want to keep asking questions that are breaking through these layers until you get to the good stuff. You want to keep asking questions until you get to the inspired motivation, that intrinsic motivation. But be warned, in asking these questions and going deeper, you are going to make people uncomfortable.

I think the quality of your sales career and the quality of your commissions, and the size of your commissions will be directly related to your ability to make people uncomfortable on a regular basis but still show empathy and care towards them. Don't flinch if your questions make somebody uncomfortable. That's what they are designed to do. That's what you're taught to do.

You must be willing to challenge people. If they give you a superficial answer about their motivation, what is compelling them to take action, it's probably going to come back as an external motivation or an identified motivation. Those are the two most common "weak sauce" motivators. They are motivators, but they're kind of feeble when it comes to you being able to make a sale. Make sure you dig deep enough until you get to the *intrinsic* motivator.

If you can't get to an intrinsic motivator through the questions you ask, you're going to struggle with your results. Some of the best salespeople I have ever worked with or currently work with understand this intuitively. But you've got to practice this stuff. You've got to know when people are serving you weak stuff and when people are serving you strong stuff.

You want to get to the strong motivators. Do they have an internal connection? Do they have an internal inspiration to do what they're asking you to help them do?

WHAT'S YOUR MOTIVATION?

As with so many things, understanding this concept fully means that you need to take a look at yourself first. I'm going to give you some examples about each of these four categories and I want you to consider how each type of motivation does or doesn't support your sales career.

If your reason, if your cause for being a sales professional is an external motivator—somebody's telling you, you got to go do this, you need to get this done—then I want you to find the empathy for yourself. I want you to find that love for what you do. I want you to get to the place where you're inspired by what you do.

That's what motivates me. I feel a tremendous amount of energy and a tremendous amount of inspiration by doing what I do. Doing sales is something that I love, I absolutely love. Don't get me wrong, though, it didn't come naturally. I actually had to develop that love for sales. I had to develop that inspiration to help me be better.

If you have an introjected type of motivation for being a salesperson, what that means is you're doing it because you feel like you should. The words 'should' and 'guilt' often show up in the same sentence, and they're almost synonymous when we talk about this type of work —you're doing it because you feel you *should*.

That might motivate you to start, but it's not good enough to sustain. You've got to let it motivate you to the point where you can be inspired, identified. If you have identified, "Hey, I need to do this because it's not getting done. I need to make money, and I need to check that off my list," it might get you there. It might get you some action, but it needs to be a bridge to get you to the place where your motivation, your motives to take action, come intrinsically, come from deep down inside of you.

When you have a great day, it's not that hard to be excited. It's not that hard to be inspired. But where you really find the growth, where you really find that happiness, and that sweet spot is when you can find inspiration in the midst of challenge. Challenge and inspiration are not two separate things. They're actually very linear in their relationship. The energy, the talent, and the skills it takes to be excited and happy are the same talents, skills, and energy it takes to overcome and conquer challenges. They're actually the same thing, with different perceived emotions surrounding them.

I want you to think of the challenges. Think about things that happen during your day. It could be that you didn't close any sales. It could be you had a bad conversation with a client. It could be nobody showed up for your appointments. It could be the leads aren't very good. These are things that could be perceived as a challenge.

When you look at these things with perspective, and you look at the grand scheme of things, these are also times you can learn from and grow from. I think if you can find that, you will find a way to perpetually motivate and inspire yourself. I can't tell you this more clearly than by saying this: When you learn or continue to practice perpetual internal motivation, that perpetual inspiration of yourself, it will bleed and ooze and spill on everyone and everything you touch.

When you have the ability, which all of us do, when you're on the phone, talking to somebody, you have the ability to connect with people emotionally. When you have the ability to inspire other people, when you are the source that stimulates and creates and compels somebody else to get into intrinsic motivation, then you're going to win. You're going to win more often than not.

As your skill set increases, the quality of your challenges will increase as well.

I heard Tony Robbins talking once about "high-quality problems." By that, he meant facing problems caused by exceeding expectations, growing, and dealing with the challenges of expecting even more of yourself. It's a higher quality of problem, but where much is given, much is required. As you expand and as you grow, so will your challenges. If you can learn how to harness those challenges and convert them into inspiration, I think that you will live a much better life while you get better and better at what you do.

KEY TAKEAWAYS

> An important element of your sales process is to ask the right questions.

> Motivation is "the motive to take action." There are four kinds of motivation and you should quickly identify that will apply to a client:

- Extrinsic or external.

- Internal.

- Introjected.

- Identified.

ACTION STEP

In your own personal life, figure out what your goals and aspirations are and try to categorize the type(s) of motivation compelling you to those goals.

There are four types of primary psychological motivations:

- What we are told to do.

- What we are inspired to do.

- What we feel guilty for not doing.

- What we know needs to get done.

➢ Your goal is to turn your client's motivation into *inspired* action.

CHAPTER 13

You Better Say It First...

It is always better to resolve objections before the client even brings them up. If you bring typical objections first, you will make them seem common and normal. In other words, the client is not the first one to feel that way. If the client brings up an objection first, you will immediately be in defensive mode, which will radically change the energy of the call. Most often, if somebody else brings up an objection first, you will find yourself in a combative and almost argumentative situation.

In the movie *8 Mile*, which is loosely based on rapper Eminem's life story, he uses this technique brilliantly. In the final scene, he is in a rap battle competition. The aim of a rap battle is for each opponent to rap about the other's weaknesses. In a genius move, Eminem spends most of his rap highlighting his OWN weaknesses. The other guy is left with nothing to say. Mic drop!

Think about this, if you're in a sales call and somebody brings up a concern, and in your mind, you're thinking, "Oh man, that always comes up, or I knew that was going to come up, or I knew that was on their mind." If that happens to you often, you need to rework things in your script, rework things in your presentation so you are prepared.

You can easily prepare for objections because I believe you already know what they are. And if you already know what they are, you need to bring them up first. You see, when you bring them up it changes the relationship of that conversation. It changes the energy of the conversation.

Let me give you some quick examples. I'm going to use the three most common objections that I hear from one day to the next. Those are time, fear, and money.

Now, what's interesting about those three objections is, typically, people only verbalize two of them. They will only verbalize two of the three top concerns. So you have to talk about that third one, which is "fear." It's the one that is least often communicated by the client. They're going to have a fear about what exactly it is they're contemplating buying.

Typically, that fear comes from feelings such as they don't know, they're worried it won't work, they're worried they're going to be taken advantage of, they're worried they're going to be scammed. These are all fear-based thoughts that will go through their head.

When I go into a call, I know there's a 90% probability that those three objections are going to come up. So what I'm going to do in my script is to cross those things off the list. I am going to bring them up, talk about them, and address them before the client has an opportunity to bring them up.

Here's an example of the client saying something first. You get to the end of a call, and you ask one of the worst questions you could ever ask. You say, "Do you have any other questions?" The person starts racking their brain, going, "Well, yeah, how much does it cost?" Then automatically, you blurt out, "Oh, well, it's $3,000."

What's your client's reaction to this? It will be, "Whoa, that's too much money." All of a sudden, you're in this weird, awkward conversation. You knew cost was going to come up as an issue, you know the concern around the price was going to come up, but you didn't get out in front of it.

So I'm going to give you some strategy and language as to how you can bring up cost before the client does so you can completely change the conversation and dynamics.

I used to do a webinar every Monday and Thursday night. I would talk to groups of people who were interested in buying a product. This product costs about $10,000. I knew that if I had 25 people on the phone, 24 of them were going to have a concern or a worry around fear, time, or money.

During my webinar, when I talked to people, I always told people during the conversation, "Now, what I'd like to do is I'd like to answer some questions you might have. But the first thing I'm going to do is answer the three questions that come up the most with the people whom I typically talk to."

The first one is time. How much time will it take to actually do what it is that you want me to do? If I'm taking an education course, if I'm doing some kind of training, how much time will it take me? I'm going to answer that question for you. The second question is cost. I mean, obviously, what we're talking about isn't free. It does cost money, so I wanted to make sure we tackle that head-on. I want to talk to you about how much it costs and what it entails, and make sure that there's a path to payment, and make sure you have an opportunity to take advantage of this.

Third, I want to talk about effort. I use the word "effort." But really, it comes down to fear because most people worry or have fear around whether they can or can't do something. I want to be very clear and give them some direct outline on how long it will take and what kind of effort it will take to do this.

TIME

Continuing my example...

Let's go back and talk about the first objection. How much time will it take? "A reasonable person who has given this a considerable amount of effort, who really takes this seriously, it will take you about an hour and a half a day to go through this course.

"Unless you're some kind of very detail-oriented engineer where you have to do things two or three times before you get it, this should take you a reasonable amount of time, an hour and a half a day, 90 minutes a day. Do you think that's something that you could carve out on a daily basis to accomplish the goals you're trying to achieve?"

I say it like that better be a yes. Rarely am I going to get somebody who says, "No, I can't carve out 90 minutes."

Think of the flip side. If they bring up the time objection first, they've already convinced themselves they don't have enough time to do it. If I bring it up first, they will agree 90 minutes is not a stretch to carve out of their normal day. Most people would exercise or commute 90 minutes a day. We do many things for 90 minutes a day that are not as important as improving ourselves. Learning a new skill set to better your life is a valuable use of your time. If you bring up that objection first, it completely and radically changes the energy in which that conversation takes place.

MONEY

Let's go on to money. Money is always a concern. Money and people's relationship with money carries a tremendous amount of energy. It can be a positive energy, or it can be a negative energy. But, typically, in conversations around cost, people have been programmed to have a very unhealthy relationship with money.

You want to talk about two concepts really quickly when it comes to money. I share these concepts with my clients before we talk about money. You want to talk about *programming*; I go through about a four-minute presentation of the difference between a consumer mindset and an investor mindset.

I say, very simply, you have a consumer mindset when you measure the thing you want to buy against what's in your bank account today. With an investor mindset, you measure the thing you want to buy against what that investment can put in your bank account in the future. If I walk into a store to buy a television, and that television costs $3,000, and I only have $1,000 in my bank account, I am going to feel that television is expensive. I'm going to have an issue with the cost.

I have that issue because I am measuring the cost of the item against what is currently at my disposal in my bank account. With a consumer mindset, that's how I measure expensive versus inexpensive. In a business sense, or with an investor mindset, that's not the way the average businessman or businesswoman thinks. The average businessperson thinks about what a purchase can produce.

If I go to a car dealership to buy a truck, and I have a business mindset, I go in, and the sales rep at the car dealership tells me the truck is $60,000. In my mind, I think, "If I buy this truck for $60,000, I can continue using it for my landscaping business; it's going to help me produce $5,000 more a month in revenue. I can have this paid back in one year. This makes sense."

Someone with an investor mindset thinks about what the purchase can produce in the future, as opposed to what is in the bank account now.

I spend about four minutes with my clients explaining these two ways of thinking. Consumer versus business or investor mindset is not a new conversation. This has been taught, regurgitated, and written about over and over for decades. But the conversation is about reminding the client that there is an alternative and smarter way to look at things.

"Are you clear on what this investment in your education can produce for you?" Shift this entire conversation to production and away from cost. Things that cost you money are heavy. They're like an anchor around your neck.

Spending money to produce something is totally different. I'll give you one example. This year, I had a goal that I was going to branch out into real estate as part of my investment portfolio.

This year, I did something I've never done before, I bought a commercial property. The thought process I went through was much different than what I would use to buy a house I would live in. When you buy a house, you don't think that much about your payback or your return on it, other than perhaps its potential for appreciation in value. The purchase is mostly about having a great place to live. Will I enjoy living in it? That might be the return.

With a commercial property, I had to really focus on what it would produce. My experience buying this commercial property was from the perspective of treating it purely as a business decision. I had to put 25% down on that commercial property. I had to put down more money out of pocket and pay a higher interest rate to get a commercial loan. I measured that entire decision based on what the property could produce as opposed to what it cost. What it did was radically shift the relationship I had with the money I was going to put into that property. It made the decision quite easy.

If you have this conversation with people about an investor versus consumer mindset, before you talk about money, you are coaching them and training them to get into an investor mindset.

Your question about money might sound like this. "John, now that we really did dive into the concept of a business or an investor mindset, based on that, when you look at the cost of our program, is that affordable for you right now? Will this produce for you what you're looking for it to produce?" If they say, "Yes, it will produce it." Then you say, "Great. Is that affordable for you at this time?" If they say no, then you go into conversations about resources.

If you exhaust all avenues they have for paying, then you can go into a conversation about funding—never financing—only funding. You "finance" things you are purchasing with a consumer mindset; you are "funding" things that you are purchasing with an investor mindset. Again, just a little change language there, but it penetrates the consciousness.

FEAR

Now, the third objection we talked about was fear. Fear wraps itself around many different things. You have all heard the acronym for fear: False Evidence Appearing Real. Most people fear what they think *could* happen. They're not afraid of what has already happened because, well. It's already happened. They might be mad about what happened. But you can't fear what's already happened. You can only fear what's in the future, or what you imagine is in the future.

Generally speaking, people only fear what they don't know. When you walk through a dark room, you're afraid of what you're going to run into. One of your jobs as a highly professional and highly ethical salesperson is to turn on the lights, make sure they know everything they need to know, make sure you've answered all their questions. Future pace your conversation.

Imagine spending 30 seconds with your client saying, "Hey John, we get a lot of people who get hung up on not making a decision about moving forward. A lot of it comes down to fear. Now in my experience, fear is only based on what we can't see in the future.

"Based on what we've talked about, based on the information you've gathered, based on the questions I've answered for you, have we wiped that fear away, John? Does the future look clear? Does the future look bright? Can you see yourself moving forward with this? Have we effectively eliminated that fear?"

Generally speaking, with that invitation, they're going to say, "Yes, you have." You're going to come back, and you're going to say, "Great."

"Because if we've taken care of how much time it takes, you've committed to doing 90 minutes a day, if we've taken care of this idea of a business expense versus a consumer expense, and we know we can help you find funding to take this project on, and we've already answered your questions, the lights are on, and you don't fear what's coming next. You're actually anxious and excited about what's coming next. John, what do you think is the next logical step to get started?"

Their answer should be to get started. The relationship changes. At this point, you can start the order process.

As soon as you have overcome those three main objections and have done so on your cadence, on your process, not on theirs, they will be ready to buy.

Saying things first is how you become the leader. It's how you take control of the conversation. If you get off a phone call, and there were no objections, there was no fear, there was no resistance to your selling process or your purchase, something's wrong. There's something they didn't tell you. Everybody has some kind of trepidation. It's human nature.

KEY TAKEAWAYS

➢ It is always better to resolve objections before the client even brings them up.

➢ The most common concerns of clients are time, fear, and money.

➢ Bringing up a client's likely concern before they do enables you to take control of the situation and build trust.

CHAPTER 14

Don't Say Too Much

The only products that sell themselves are in the grocery store! That is why grocery stores don't employ salespeople. They employ cashiers.

If you are working with a lead who has inquired about your product, they are already interested and have proven it by inquiring. Don't let them act like they are not interested. Your job, as a salesperson, is to compel someone to make a *decision*.

Oftentimes this is the hardest thing to get someone to do. Most inexperienced salespeople will end a call with no decision being made by the potential client. This is fatal! The probability of you getting a second chance to talk to them is greatly decreased if you hang up the phone without getting a decision.

YOU CAN GET TRIPPED UP BY KNOWING TOO MUCH

I want to talk about a trap that new salespeople often fall into. That trap is knowing too much and then responding to a client's questions with too much information.

179

In the beginning, you don't know much, but then you go to more training. You learn much more about your product. After about the first month, all of a sudden, you have this massive treasure trove of information about your product.

If you're selling a software product, you'll know all the intricate details of how it works. If you're selling an education product, you'll know everything about each course. The challenge behind that is all of a sudden, now, you're smarter. Well, not smarter. You have more *knowledge*. You have more product knowledge. All of a sudden, you fall into a trap. You fall into a habit of sharing everything you know about the product because the more knowledge you have, the more information you start feeding to your customers.

I could wrap up this entire chapter in three words. Those three words are: Just. Shut. Up. You need to practice the art of saying more with fewer words. I'm going to tell you how to fix the problem of saying too much just because you know a lot. It's not just about brevity. It's not just about giving short answers. It's not about being concise. I'm going to tell you the two things your customer wants.

In the beginning of your sales career, you may think customers want all the answers. You think they want to know how something works. You think they want all the details. But people don't buy things on logic. People buy things on emotion, and then they support their emotion-driven decision with logic. However, they trick you. They ask you questions that lead you to believe they want to know all the details. I'm here to tell you, they don't need all the details and they don't want all the details. Here's what they want. They want two things. They want to know, "Does it work?" and, "Can I do it?" Those are the only two things they need to know about the product. Does it work and can I do it?

The "Does it work?" part—this is where you're going to use some examples. If somebody asks you, "Does it work?" you could simply say, "Yes, absolutely," and then move on. Okay, they want to know, "Does it work? Can I do it?"

WHAT THEY REALLY WANT TO KNOW

At one point in my career, I used to be in the higher education space, selling enrollment for one of the largest private universities in North America.

When I first started, I did great. I was the number one salesperson on the team. I was doing well, getting many promotions and accolades. And then, all of a sudden, my numbers went down. The reason why my numbers went down was that I started learning. I started learning more about the product.

What ended up happening was somebody would say to me on the phone, "Hey, Ryan, tell me how this works." I'll tell you right now, if anybody ever says to you, "Tell me how it works," it's a trick! They don't even know they are tricking you.

I'm going to do a sidestep, just a minute, to talk about human psychology and human communication.

There's something you need to understand. The average person does not know how to ask for what they want. Most people do not know how or are embarrassed or fearful to ask for what they want. You're going to find this in business. You're going to find this in your personal relationships as well.

In your personal relationships, somebody might ask you for something, and you might tell them, and then they get mad because it's not really what they wanted to know. You're confused. You think, "Wait a minute, but that's what you asked me, right?"

You need to practice. You need to find these trigger questions people typically don't know how to ask. This is a good example. They say, "Tell me how it works," or "How does it work?" Now, I'm going to tell you they don't care. They don't care how it works. What that question actually means is... "Can I do it?"

When I worked for the university, I would be on the phone talking to prospective students. We were a 100% online university. At the time, we were the pioneer. Nobody was doing it like we were doing it. We were delivering education services to hundreds of thousands of people. The traditional university delivers to perhaps thousands of students. So, we had cracked a code. We had figured out a way to deliver accredited educational programs and degree programs online all over the world. When I first started, I didn't really understand how it worked, But I did really well with enrolling people.

After a while, when people started saying, "Tell me how it works. How does it work?" I fell into the trap of trying to share too much because I had figured it out. I had learned how it worked.

The instructional process was based on using Newsgroups. I started explaining to people exactly how Newsgroups worked. I said, "You can log in at any time. Your instructor could be in Germany. You could be in California. Because it's asynchronous, you guys can participate at different times." I started describing how all of this works, because after all, they asked me, "How does it work?" I was being kind, and I was being responsible. I was answering their question.

What a mistake. My enrollments and my sales went to the floor. That's when I learned that nobody cares. So, once I figured that out, once I figured that nobody cares how it works, what I realized is that all they want to know is, "Can I do it?" So, I changed the description I used so it focused on getting them to understand they could do it.

The next time someone asked me how it worked, here's what I said to them. I said, "Hey, John, do you use email?" He would say, "Yes, I do."

"If I sent you an email, could you reply to it and send it back to me?" He would say, "Yeah, I can do that." Listen to the words, *"I can do that."*

"If I sent you an email that had an attachment, could you open it?" His answer would be, "Yes, I can do that." Can you hear the programming going on here?

Then the next question I asked was, "Can you send me an email with an attachment on it?" He would say, "Yes, I can do that."

I got the student to say, "I can do that" three times! My final description of the product was, "John, it's exactly like that. If you can do those three things, you can do this."

That was my entire product description. I asked three questions. The answer to each of the questions was, "I can do that." It was relatable. It was something he did every day. He knows how to use email. So, he can send and receive. He knows how to open and close attachments. That's all it really took to participate in our classroom.

When I started doing that, when I started using those three questions, I always got the same reply for each question: "Yes, I can do that." My follow-up response would always be, "Then you can do this."

The question was, "How does it work?" The answer was, "You can do this." You see the logic?

Don't be led like a horse with a bit in your mouth by the questions they ask. Don't think, "Well, they asked me how it works. I better tell them." No, not only do they not need to know how it works, they don't know how your sales process works. Only you know that.

When they ask you those types of questions, quickly be able to decipher what they're really asking you. This is just one example. Product knowledge does not have to be shared. I think you should learn everything you can about your product, where it came from, what it does, statistically, what outcomes it has. I think you should have all that information in your back pocket, because, every once in a while, it's valuable. But I would not use the reams of information you have in your head to describe your product because you are going to make somebody's head explode. And that's not conducive to making a sale!

Make difficult things seem simple, and you're going to win.

A really good way to do this is to slow down and get clarification. If somebody asks you a question and you think, "Oh, this might be one of those traps that Ryan was talking about. This might be one of those times when they're not really asking me what they want to know," take a deep breath. Ask them to repeat the question. If it comes out the same way, tell them to restate it. *I'm not quite sure I understand what you're asking. Can you ask that again?*

By the third time that you ask them to repeat it, they're going to come back with simplicity, brevity, a succinct question. You're going to be able to say, "Oh, okay. That's what you wanted to know. Okay." If you do that, you're going to have a ton of success.

KEY TAKEAWAYS

➢ Your job, as a salesperson, is to compel someone to make a *decision*.

➢ Ending a call with no decision being made by the potential client is FATAL!

➢ A powerful sales tool is these three words: Just. Shut. Up. Often sales success comes from saying less.

➢ People don't buy things on logic; people buy things on emotion.

➢ The average person does not know how to ask for what they want. You need to find the trigger questions people typically don't know how to ask.

CHAPTER 15

Pitch Perfect

Are you a Closer or a Cashier?

A sales conversation without a clear and specific invitation or call to action is not a sales conversation. You are either doing customer support or sales. Don't spend an hour of your time with a potential client without asking for the sale.

Cashiers just collect money; they don't sell. A professional salesperson connects with a client on an emotional level, answers their questions, diagnoses their needs and problems, offers solutions to those problems, and has a confident and definitive call to action.

The pitch, the close, the call to action, the wrap-up! Yes, we call it many things, and most newer sales reps think the invitation to buy comes as this big grand one-liner at the end of the call that gets everyone to buy. Not exactly. It is true, to close a sale you must make a direct invitation to buy the product. However, this is not a one-time thing that culminates at the end of the call.

Remember, either you're selling them or they're selling you. Who is going to close whom? I don't want this to sound like it's a battle. A really good salesperson creates an environment where the customer can be inspired to buy something. A poor salesperson is going to create an environment where the person has to be *sold.*

There's a big, energetic difference between a customer who is buying because they've been inspired versus somebody who has been forced or coerced into a sale. One of my favorite sayings I like to share with people is this:

"We should not be twisting arms; we should be holding hands."

The term "closing the sale" originates from the real estate industry. When you finalize the purchase of a piece of property, you sign what are called "closing documents." A home or land or a building is not sold until the buyer signs the closing documents.

However, I'd like to encourage you to change the language you use when it comes to closing a sale, because I don't think that "close," in terms of a sale, has a super positive energy. I don't think it has a positive impact. In fact, could you say it to your customer? Could you get on the phone with your customer and say, "Hey, I'm really hoping to close you." It sounds like a forceful thing, right? It sounds awkward. If you can't say it to your customer, then it's probably language you should change in your vocabulary, in your mind, so you can create a better environment—an environment in which they *want* to buy from you.

The three most impactful points, the three most powerful moments in your entire conversation with your customer, are going to be your opening statement, the description of your product, and your invitation for them to purchase. Those three components should be written, they should be rehearsed, they should be practiced, they should be tested, they should be evaluated, you should memorize them. Those three things should be the most powerful moments of your entire phone call.

OPENING STATEMENT

You should not re-create your introduction every time you pick up the phone. Don't go for originality. When I used to work on inbound leads, one of the things I used to always say in my opening statement was, "Hi, this is Ryan calling from ABC Co. You had requested us to give you a call." Because when they inquired, they did just that; they requested us to make a call. I always said, "You requested us to give you a call." I didn't get pushback from the customer of, "Why are you calling me?"

DESCRIPTION

Your product description should be clear, concise, and resolve the problem the person is looking to resolve. Your description of the product should be so clear and so scripted that when you say it, it comes out as one of the strongest statements you could possibly make. "John, now I'm going to describe to you how our product works."

You're not going to go detail for detail, you're not going to spend much time, and you're only going to say what matters. You're not going to go through and describe every aspect and every tenet of the product. Again, you're only going to describe what *matters*. But you are going to do it in a way that has enthusiasm. You are going to have a confident tone in your voice.

INVITATION TO PURCHASE

Your invitation to purchase (that thing you used to call "the closing statement") needs to be practiced; it needs to be written. Your invitation to purchase the product should be scripted, and it should be the same thing every single time. You should use it so often and so repetitively that it becomes the only version of your invitation because the more you use it, the stronger it becomes.

Examples of Invitations to Purchase

Let's give you some examples of things you could say that are powerful.

I want to make sure you understand why I want it scripted. Your invitation to purchase the product should be your goal. It should be your goal as to what you want to accomplish with this particular customer. Do you know what your goal is as you're talking to somebody? We talked about a script and an outline. In that outline, we said, "I'm going to ask you a few questions, I'm going to answer all of your questions, I'm going to describe my product to you, and we are going to see if this is a good fit."

I used to say that on every single phone call. In the very beginning of my call, my opening statement, my introduction of me setting expectations, I would say, "We are going to see if this is a good fit for you." I use that language because that language shows up in my invitation at the very end. I'm going to give you some examples of invitations you can use on the phone, and you can practice these.

You should practice your statements until they become second nature for you, until they become a strength for you. The reason why I said, 'if this is a good fit' at the beginning is because my invitation at the end was always, "John, do you think this is a good fit for you?" It was not an accident I connected my opening expectation statement to my final invitation statement. I wanted to plant an expectation in the person's subconscious in the first couple of minutes of our phone call how this call was going to end.

After I've taken them through my sales journey, I am going to ask them, "John, do you feel like this is a good fit for you?" If John says yes, you open an order form, and you go right in and take an order. If John says no, your next question is, "Okay, let's talk about it. What doesn't fit?" Then you will find out some specifics on what you can go through and start overcoming some objections. You can start going through some further conversation. That's the way I used to do it.

Let me give you some examples of other ways you can do it. Again I hope this helps give you some language, some how-to ideas, and some guidance to create your own invitation statement.

One of my other favorites you can use is, "John, we have gone through all the information. I have asked you all the questions I need. I've answered all of your questions. It sounds like this is a good fit for you." Then here it comes, "John, what do you think is the next logical step to move forward?"

There are reasons why I use those words. I didn't just decide it one day, but that statement came about after much practice, altering and fidgeting with language, and fiddling with words. When you say, "What do you think is the next logical step?" they already know what the next logical step is. In fact, the word 'no' is not the next logical step, and they know that. When you ask them, what's the next logical step, the only logical step if everything lines up the way we described it is to go ahead and get started on ordering.

The golden rule is that I always set things up, I always set things up ahead of time, so they're prepared for what I'm about to ask them. You can use this dialogue, too: "John,

I've asked you everything I need to ask. I've answered everything you've had for me. After describing our product to you, it sounds like this is a perfect fit for you." Then for my invitation statement, I would say, "John, as a representative of ABC Co, I'd like to officially invite you to join our program. Will you accept my invitation?"

If they say yes, then you are going to open an order form. You will not communicate anything else about the product, you will not answer any other questions, you will not pass go, you will immediately just start taking an order. When you get a yes, the relationship changes. When somebody says, "Yes, I would accept it," the relationship changes at that point. You are no longer a salesperson at that point. You have done the sales job, you have compelled them, and they have made a decision. They said yes.

Go Into Order-taker Mode

Immediately after they say yes, you are now an order taker. You are now a cashier. When you go to the grocery store to buy a gallon of milk, does the cashier turn to you and say, "Did you have any questions about this gallon of milk?"

Does the cashier turn to you and say, "Are you sure you want to buy this?"

Does the cashier pick up your gallon of milk and say, "Oh, this company is fantastic. They pasteurize their milk. It's homogenized. It's fortified with Vitamin D."

If they did that, you'd be annoyed, right? Because you already chose to buy it!

Think about that when you're in a sales capacity. "Will you accept my invitation?" When they say, "Yes," close your mouth, the sales job is over. You are now a cashier.

Immediately go into process mode, go into transaction mode, start collecting information. Whether it be a name, an address, credit card number, whatever it is, immediately go down that path and don't start overselling. When you oversell, that is known as "selling beyond the sale." Don't do it. Just wrap it up. Take the order.

These are three examples of ways you can create an environment where somebody *wants* to buy from you, as opposed to you twisting an arm. If you have to pull your customer across the finish line, that's going to be a really awkward situation, and they're not going to enjoy the process.

If you're on their side of the table and you're working on this together, then you're looking for a solution to the problems they have. You're looking for a solution to the challenge they're having. Once you determine if your solution is a match and it can resolve their issues, you're going to make an official invitation for them to join your program.

Now, whatever language you choose, you have to choose something. Some salespeople get anxious when it's time to ask for money. They get so nervous that what they say doesn't come out with confidence. It doesn't come out as a matter of process. It comes out as an option. When you ask the question, you need to ask it in a way that doesn't leave any other perceived option.

It is what it is; it's time to get started. "John, based on what we've talked about, based on what you've told me, this looks like a perfect fit for you. Let's go ahead and get you started." You can just ask your invitation question then. "What do you think is the next logical step?" Or ask any other ones we talked about. You're going to find that confidence sometimes is going to inspire people in a way. It's going to move them into a sale.

Conversely, can you hear the difference in this close? You go to wrap up, and you go to invite somebody, and you say, "Well, John, it looks like I've answered all your questions. So, what do you think?" I can't think of any-thing being worse than this. It's the worst thing you can say on the phone. "What do you think?"

All of a sudden, you've asked your client to start thinking, you've asked them to start thinking about options, you've invited them to think about objections. You're asking them to open this can of worms that you don't want to be opened. If you've done your job correctly, if you've done it pro-fessionally, then you should be able to go in and just say, "John, it looks like it's a great fit. I would like to officially invite you to join our program. Will you accept my invita-tion?" And you can move forward.

It's Like Proposing

You should write down your invitation and polish and prac-tice it. You should go to somebody and ask them to listen to it. You should say it over and over; it should not be clunky. It shouldn't be too wordy; it should come out very fluently and eloquently. It should be something you've said a mil-lion times or something that sounds like you've said it a million times. Once you get that closing statement down, you're going to benefit greatly. Hopefully, some of my ideas will help you develop your own invitation.

If you have an invitation you're using right now, and it's not getting the results you need, then change it. Start wordsmithing, start looking at every single word in that closing statement, and see if it's impactful, see if it's inviting, and see if it means what it's intended to mean. Make sure as you're going through your closing statement, your official invitation, that it is deliberate. It is designed to *finalize* a conversation. It is designed to take your customer to the closing documents for them to sign. That's how it should end.

Your entire conversation should be built on the idea that you're going to change the relationship at some point in this conversation, and you're going to invite them to join your program. Everything you say should culminate in this invitation.

Imagine you are dating somebody, you've been on two dates with them, but you don't yet know too much about them. During dinner on your third date, you say, "So, what do you think?" They're going to look at you like, "About what? What do you mean?" "Well, do you want to get married?"

Would you ever propose to somebody unless you already knew all the information you needed to know? Would you propose to somebody if you didn't already know the answer? Think about that one. They say attorneys only ask questions they already know the answer to. I would encourage you to follow that same practice. The answer to your official invitation should never come as a surprise to you.

For those of you who are married or in some kind of committed relationship, could you imagine going into a proposal thinking to yourself, oh, gosh, I know I just spent $20,000 on this ring, I wonder what they're going to say? Are you going to play a "numbers game" and hope your conversion is at least 20%? Ridiculous, right? You are absolutely shooting for a 100% close rate on your proposal. You should already know the answer.

In a sales call, keep this in mind. You should be able to ask all the questions. You should be able to answer all of their questions. You should be able to give such a thorough product description that the next logical step they're expecting, and you're expecting, is that you are going to propose to them, you're going to officially invite them to join your program. This is an effective way to do sales. This is an effective way to wrap things up at the end.

I'm going to warn you about some clients out there. You may think because you had a good phone call, you made a sale. Sometimes your customer is going to say yes to everything you say just to get you off the phone. Sometimes they're going to agree to everything, and you're going to think, 'Oh, I'm having a great phone call!' But a great phone call can be measured very easily. How? Propose to them! If you ever want to know where you stand with your customer, propose to them, and you'll find out really quickly where you stand.

Talking Price

One other bit of language you have to adopt and practice concerns price. The price can be a very awkward part of your conversation, and sometimes salespeople don't like to ask for $1,000, or $2,000, or $5,000, or $30,000. Sometimes, salespeople have a weird relationship with money, too, where they struggle to ask other people for money.

One of the strategies I used to use in the past when I was on the phone was the way I would go over the price with somebody. Hypothetically, let's say my product costs $5,000. That's a pretty average round number for big-ticket sales. If my product cost $5,000, and a customer asked said, "How much does it cost?" I would say, "Well, here's what you get, and the cost of the program is $5,000."

Before they could react—I didn't put a period after $5,000, I would put a comma—I would say, "Our program costs $5,000, now, John, considering your current financial situation, is this affordable for you?" I don't want to know anything else at this point. I just want to know, do you have it or do you not have it? That's a very polite and professional way to ask.

"John, considering your financial situation right now, is that affordable for you?" If John says yes, then go into your invitation. "Great. John, I'd like to officially invite you to join our program. Will you accept my invitation?" If John says no, then you're going to go into a conversation about finances and about money and about funding and about resource challenges, which you should have already done.

Another option for you, as you get close to the end of your call, is that even if you've already talked about price, if you told them 15 minutes ago that the cost of the program was $12,000, and they're still on the line with you, and they know the price, and you've gone through and edified, and you've supported, and you've created a value proposition that's at least 20 times the value of the product, then you come back around, and you say, "John, I know I told you the cost of the program was $12,000. Considering your financial situation right now, is that affordable for you?" At that point, you play the shut-up game.

The shut-up game is where you close your mouth. You're not allowed to say something after you ask that question. Simple.

"Is it affordable for you?" You don't talk until they talk.

That's a yes or no question. If they say anything other than yes or no, then you're going to have a conversation on your hands. If they say no, you don't then say, "Tell me more about that."

What one person thinks is affordable isn't the same definition as what somebody else thinks is affordable. So, if they say no, ask them, "What do you mean by that?" They're going to say, "Well, I can't afford it right now. But I can on Friday when I get my tax return."

If they say, "No, it's not affordable." You say, "What do you mean by that?" or, "Tell me more about that" They might then say, "Well, I can't pay for it right now, but I can in my next paycheck."

Then you can talk about a path to payment, and that's a whole different conversation.

The Recap

Always focus most of your practice and attention on the three most important elements of your sales conversation: your opening statement, your product description, and your invitation.

Remember, for the strongest invitation to purchase, make your intentions very clear in the beginning of the call.

Let's recap the examples of invitations to purchase.

Example #1

(During introduction) John, today I will be asking you some questions. I will be answering all of your questions, I will tell you all about our product/service, and we will see if this is a good fit for you. Fair enough?

(I have just told them in my introduction that the end goal is to see if this is a good fit...)

(The wrap up) John, now that we have been through all the information, I can tell by your answers and your goals that is a good fit for you, will you agree? Yes! Great, let's get you started!

Example #2

John, after learning more about what you are looking for, it sounds like our product checks all your boxes. What do you think is the next logical step?

Example #3

John, it appears that our product/service fits your needs quite well. As a representative of the company, I would like to officially invite you to join our program. Will you accept my invitation? Yes! Great, let's get you started.

Example #4

John, our program costs 'X' dollars. Considering your current financial situation, is that affordable for you at this time?

Now that you, the reader, have learned about the *calls to action*, as the author of the book, I'd like to officially invite you to take the next logical step and turn the page (smiley face).

KEY TAKEAWAYS

➢ A sales conversation has to have a clear and specific invitation or call to action.

➢ To close a sale, you must make a direct invitation to buy the product.

➢ Create an environment where the customer is inspired to buy something, not an environment in which the person has to be *sold*.

➢ **Remember:** "We should not be twisting arms; we should be holding hands."

Change your vocabulary: "Closing" to "Invitation to Purchase."

➢ **Do** rehearse the three Power Moments of your sales pitch:

- Opening Statement.

- Product Description.

- Invitation to Purchase.

➢ **Don't** "sell beyond the sale." Wrap it up. Take the order.

CHAPTER 16

Double-A's

For any sales process that requires more than one touch with a client, always end a call with a double-A. This is textbook basic sales practice. What's a double-A?

An Appointment and an Assignment.

If a follow-up customer touch is needed, the customer should know when they will speak with you next and what they should be doing in the meantime. The appointment should only be booked far enough in advance to allow enough time to finish the assignment. Here are some examples:

➤ Assignment: Talk to spouse. Appointment: Next day.

➤ Assignment: Transfer money from 401k. Appointment: End of the week or within 5 days.

➤ Assignment: Do some research. Appointment: Next day

> ➤ <u>Assignment</u>: Think about it. <u>Appointment</u>: Same day.

KEY TAKEAWAYS

> ➤ If a follow-up customer touch is needed, always end a call with the Double-A's.

> ➤ Appointment.

> ➤ Assignment.

ACTION STEP

On your next sales call, end the call by setting up the next appointment with your client and give them an assignment. For example, the assignment could be "talk to your spouse" or "transfer money from your 401K."

CHAPTER 17

Conclusion

Whew! We've gone through quite a journey together! Thank you for taking the time to let me guide you, and I should also say CONGRATULATIONS! Congratulations that you took that next step into learning about sales. You put aside the time; you put in some effort. So, well done for that. As you've learned, it's hard for customers to make a decision to commit. And in some way, you *are* a customer who decided to commit.

We've covered many topics and elements of a successful sales process, and it is my hope that I've explained things in a way that has moved you further ahead in your sales journey. If you follow the steps, techniques, tips, and strategies as I've presented them and apply them as you gain experience, you'll be a highly skilled (not to mention well-paid) salesperson in no time!

Sales takes perseverance. It takes time to perfect your pitch. It takes fortitude to weather the "no's" as you build up your experience and refine your script. Need some inspiration. Here are some of my favorite quotes that I look to when I need some inspiration to soldier on:

"Our greatest weakness lies in giving up. The most certain way to succeed is always to try just one more time." – *Thomas Edison*

"Become the person who would attract the results you seek." – *Jim Cathcart*

"Don't watch the clock; do what it does. Keep going." – *Sam Levenson*

"The secret of getting ahead is getting started." – *Mark Twain*

"Quality performance starts with a positive attitude." – *Jeffrey Gitomer*

"Your attitude, not your aptitude, will determine your altitude." - *Zig Ziglar*

And finally, Master Yoda seems to have a wise word on pretty much everything, sales included!

"Many of the truths that we cling to depend on our point of view" – *Yoda*

You're now equipped with the tools to be a powerful salesperson. I wish you all the success in the world. I'm a salesperson, after all, so my natural instinct is to end with a call to action. So here it is:

"In the beginning of this book, I told you that I would teach you how to be an effective salesperson. I've noticed that you've stayed with me until the end of the book, and that tells me that you're interested and committed to becoming a master of sales. Am I correct that I hear a little excitement in your voice? Great! As the author of this book, I'd like to officially welcome you to get out there and start selling!"

If this book has inspired you to learn more about how to learn the skill of selling, please visit my website and inquire about our training programs and employment opportunities. We have advanced-level training and resources to accelerate your sales career. If you are new to the profession or a seasoned vet just looking to level up a bit, please reach out and see what we can do together! Cheers!

VISIT: www.J10.com